ISBN-13: 078-0-9909769-0-5

Cover and book design by Rule29

This book is dedicated to all of those who have explored conscious leadership before us and all of those who are joining us now in the great conversation.

TABLE OF CONTENTS

PART I   INTRODUCTION

i   **PREFACE**

1   **TWO LIVES**

13   **LEADING FROM ABOVE THE LINE**

PART II   THE 15 COMMITMENTS

44   **COMMITMENT 1 >**   Taking Radical Responsibility

60   **COMMITMENT 2 >**   Learning Through Curiosity

80   **COMMITMENT 3 >**   Feeling All Feelings

106 **COMMITMENT 4 >**   Speaking Candidly

134 **COMMITMENT 5 >**   Eliminating Gossip

152 **COMMITMENT 6 >**   Practicing Integrity

174 **COMMITMENT 7 >**   Generating Appreciation

188 **COMMITMENT 8 >**   Excelling in Your Zone of Genius

204 **COMMITMENT 9 >**   Living a Life of Play and Rest

224 **COMMITMENT 10 >**   Exploring the Opposite

236 **COMMITMENT 11 >**   Sourcing Approval,
                           Control and Security

252 **COMMITMENT 12 >**   Having Enough of Everything

266 **COMMITMENT 13 >**   Experiencing the World as an Ally

278 **COMMITMENT 14 >**   Creating Win for All Solutions

290 **COMMITMENT 15 >**   Being the Resolution

PART III   SHIFTING TO CONSCIOUS LEADERSHIP

302 **THE CHANGE FORMULA**

322 **NEXT STEPS**

328 **A FINAL APPRECIATION**

330 **RESOURCE LIST**

338 **WHO WE ARE**

340 **INDEX**

ACKNOWLEDGMENTS

Most of the ideas in this book we got from others. We want to first acknowledge Gay and Kathlyn Hendricks who introduced us to the power of conscious commitments and who were our original teachers for many of these concepts. We also want to acknowledge Hale Dwoskin who has guided us into the experience of "As Me" and Byron Katie who invites us over and over again to question our beliefs. Leah Pearlman created all of the comics for this book and in addition to being a collaborator on the book she is a partner with us in the great dance. Sandra Jonas brought her gifts of editing to us every step of the way and Kate Ludeman pushed us in a loving way to write a "real" book and not just a pamphlet.

The design geniuses at Rule29 took the time to really understand us and what we are up to in the world and then created a look and feel that matched it. Bringing a book to market, and launching all the parts of a movement, is like birthing a baby, and Amy Humble and Sue Barlow of Humble Barlow have been fantastic midwives demonstrating both mastery of their craft and unbridled enthusiasm for the project and us. We want to appreciate all of our clients who have practiced living these commitments day in and day out in the real world. Finally, to those who have been in the Conscious Leadership Group Forum for the last three years, we thank you. You have been allies, friends, learning partners, and most of all, great adventurers willing to risk everything for your full aliveness.

PREFACE

Why another book on leadership?

When we asked ourselves this question, we answered, "Because most of the current models of leadership aren't working."

We want to be clear about what we mean. Today's leadership models can achieve certain desired ends quite effectively, such as creating shareholder value, increasing market share, developing new products, beating the competition, giving certain leaders fortune and fame, and giving business schools useful frameworks for training future leaders.

But we have found that these outcomes are not enough because the models are unsustainable on three critical levels.

PERSONAL LEVEL

Our clients range from the top banks and investment firms in the world to leading healthcare organizations and the most cutting-edge technology firms. We work with entrepreneurial start-ups, small businesses, and Fortune 500 organizations. We've coached, facilitated, and consulted with thousands of leaders, including the brightest millennials and baby boomers hailed as best in class.

Many of these incredibly gifted, driven, passionate, and purposeful leaders are fraying at the edges. One Fortune 500 CEO reported to us recently that his equally competent physician wife was shocked at the number of wildly successful twentysomethings who were requesting prescriptions for Xanax and Ambien via text messages because they had no time to come in for an appointment. We've worked with many astounding leaders who enter midlife with broken marriages, fractured families, hardened hearts, and dreamless futures. They can boast many quarters of beating earnings estimates and they have the money to show for it, but they're struggling to find purpose, satisfaction, happiness, and balance.

ORGANIZATIONAL LEVEL

Burned-out, stressed-out, and frazzled leaders foster organizations that experience high turnover, low employee engagement, steep healthcare costs, and dysfunctional teams that often work against one another. The current models of leadership require organizations to motivate their people largely with fear and extrinsic rewards. Though no one argues that these forms of motivation can produce short-term results, they are usually accompanied by distrust and cynicism in the workplace, which have long-term negative consequences. In this scenario, leaders must continuously ratchet up the fear and anxiety to raise productivity and then use increased monetary incentives to keep scared, cynical, and fed-up people on board. These models are simply not sustainable if the goal is to build vibrant, creative, and profitable organizations with engaged, productive teams over the long run.

The organizations that follow the conscious leadership model are winning the talent war. Once people recognize that there are companies using higher forms of motivation like intrinsic reward, play, and even love, they gravitate toward them. Further, conscious leadership organizations attract the best and brightest by leveraging each individual's unique genius capacities. They transform average workers into outstanding contributors, who in turn, help create impressive organizational results.

According to the *Chicago Tribune* and *Crain's Chicago Business*, the two best companies to work at in Chicago are Athletico and Centro. Both companies practice most of the 15 Commitments of Conscious Leadership, a model which is proving to be sustainable, self-rejuvenating, and reinforcing. Sandy Weill, former CEO and Chairman of Citigroup, once said, "What is culture except something you find in yogurt?" We disagree. Culture is the secret sauce—or lethal bacteria—of all teams. Conscious leadership cultures build success in real and concrete ways you will read about in this book.

PLANETARY LEVEL

Most current models are built on beliefs of scarcity and win/lose competition—a deeply rooted, flawed mindset found in most cultures and leaders. Like fear, this view motivates people for a while but it doesn't last. The "not enough resources" belief (money, time, energy, space, and love) and the "I/we are not enough" belief create a zero-sum game, generating winners and losers, haves and have-nots. Because we are afraid there isn't enough for all of us, we harm the planet and each other, an unworkable approach that won't sustain future generations.

So we offer this book to the great leadership conversation because we believe models like Conscious Leadership are those of present and future pioneers, who will take themselves, their organizations, and the global community to new heights of success. Conscious Leadership presents a radically new and meaningful paradigm that enhances and enriches everyone who embraces it.

We welcome all you pioneers on this journey with us.

TWO LIVES

It's 5:15 a.m. and Tim is up and at 'em. He sets his phone alarm each night but hasn't needed it for nearly four years. His phone and laptop recharge all night long on the table next to his bed. A while ago he gave into his wife's complaints and agreed to turn the ringers off but he leaves them on "vibrate," and vibrate and flash they do... all night.

Like many leaders, Tim exists on five to six hours of so-called sleep. We refer to it that way because if you actually measured his sleep, you would discover that very little of it is deep and restorative. Tim is sleep deprived and doesn't even recognize it.

"No problem," declares Tim. "I'll sleep when I'm dead!" Wandering to the bathroom a bit bleary eyed, he begins scanning his emails for anything that has blown up or could blow up. By 5:17, he has already gotten a solid jolt of his favorite chemical cocktail: adrenaline. His head is in the game. Downstairs, he brews up a double espresso and checks the morning papers and news outlets on his laptop. His adrenaline, combined with his ever-present anxiety, brings his attention to the news with a laser-beam focus most often seen in world-class athletes.

Today's a good day because Tim has time for a workout. He has never really been out of shape since his days as a competitive college athlete but rarely does he hit his target of six workouts a week. These days he says if he's "lucky," he gets three.

After exercising and taking a shower, he wakes his kids. This is an especially good day because he'll share a rare breakfast with them before catching the train to work. Tim loves his kids. In fact, his kids keep him connected to what he says really matters to him. During breakfast, though, he is half-present at best as he handles several critical emails and makes a short but "urgent" call.

A fast goodbye, hugs all around, and a peck on his wife's cheek and he is out the door. Twenty years ago, the goodbye kiss included a moment of looking into each other's eyes and a teasing touch that said "I'll be back for more later," but those days are gone. What was once an openhearted, loving connection is now a functional relationship between two people who co-parent, grow their assets, keep up their image, and occasionally check out who might be a better option.

On the train and in the game, Tim responds to emails and makes quick, determined calls. His juices are flowing— this is what he loves. Sure, the scorecard is fortune and fame, freedom and opportunity, but the game itself is all that matters. It's about being on the edge, constantly being challenged and challenging others. He feels alive. Unfortunately, Tim, and many leaders like him, can't tell the difference between being "fully alive" and feeling a mixture of adrenaline, caffeine, sugar, pressure, compulsivity, addiction, and competition, all driven by deeply repressed fear and insecurity. This shows up in many ways in Tim's life, perhaps most significantly in his inability to be by himself in silence. He can be by himself (he actually likes that), but when alone, he watches TV, reads, listens to music, does projects—anything that keeps him from facing the stillness, the emptiness, and himself.

When Tim gets to the office, the other players join him on the field and the game escalates. His team is one of the best in the industry. Their motto is "If you don't work on Saturday, don't bother coming in on Monday." They epitomize type As with their drive and competitive juice. Team meetings are intellectual sword fights where everyone is invested in being right and proving it. Mistakes are frowned upon and often covered up. Blame is the order of the day.

This anxiety is hidden and never discussed. In fact, no member of Tim's team, including Tim, would ever admit to being afraid or nervous, let alone scared or sad. Feelings are never mentioned and, except for anger, are seen as a sign of weakness. Though, in a rare honest moment, they admit to themselves that they're growing weary of the game.

Because of this environment, Tim and the other leaders have become master "spinners." They would protest this description, clinging tightly to their belief that they never lie (even though they do). But deep down, they would acknowledge that they rarely expose all their relevant thoughts and opinions. They keep their cards close to their vest because in this game, information is power and influence comes from managing people by manipulating perception.

At the end of the day, Tim grabs a beer with a couple of his closest allies. This post-game debriefing ritual is filled with celebration, strategy, storytelling, and a big dose of gossip. Much of the time is spent talking about people who aren't at the bar, and most of them know that if they don't return the next night, they'll be the target of conversation. Gossip, they maintain, is the glue that builds alliances.

Tim catches the 7:20 train back to the suburbs and works his email all the way. He's home by 8:30 just in time to kiss the kids good night, eat some pizza while watching ESPN and have a few cocktails. The drinks are important. They begin the process of bringing Tim "down" from the high that has been coursing through his veins since early in the day. Sometimes alcohol isn't enough and he'll take a pill or smoke a joint. His goal is to shut off his mind. Sleep finally comes around midnight. The alarm is set, the devices charging and buzzing and blinking.

It's been another good day.

Tim is a highly successful leader.

Tim is an unconscious leader.

Sharon's day begins with a gentle waking from a great night's sleep, followed by five minutes of intentional deep breathing and stretching. After a cup of tea, she meditates for twenty minutes. When her significant other returns from his morning jog, she meets him in the family room and they connect for a few minutes of authentic sharing and appreciation. They check to see if anything is blocking their closeness. This is Sharon's second long-term adult relationship. Her first ended in divorce, and she is committed to having a close, loving, and playful partnership that supports them both in bringing their greatest gifts to the world. It's working. It isn't without moments of drama, but they have learned to shift skillfully from being "stuck" to flowing in a supportive, creative way.

Her two kids are up by 7:00 and the entire family meets for breakfast at 7:30. The kids are now in first and third grade and like most kids they lead full, active lives. Sharon is deeply committed to being present when she is with her kids at breakfast. She makes a clear distinction between being with her kids and being present with her kids. She does both but breakfast is a time to be fully present, no TV, no computers, no communication devices. She credits her meditation practice with giving her the ability to bring her full attention to her family and if her mind wanders she brings it back to the moment.

At 8:00, Sharon is picked up by her driver and arrives at the office forty-five minutes later. She is dedicated to spending her time doing what she is uniquely gifted to do, which corresponds to what brings her the greatest joy and allows her to make her deepest contribution to the world. She calls it "living in her genius." Driving is not a genius area for her, so she has chosen to hire someone to perform that task. At first this seemed like an extravagance, but now she experiences it as marvelously supportive.

During the car ride, she opens her laptop to her "system." Several years ago, Sharon mastered David Allen's approach in his book *Getting Things Done: The Key to Stress-Free Productivity* and set up a management system that organizes everything in one location. In a matter of minutes, she can switch from her life purpose, to her current active projects, to twelve-month goals, to roles and responsibilities, to areas of focus, and to action items. Sharon doesn't use her mind to try to keep track of her complex life but rather to do what a mind is good at: thinking creatively, daydreaming, figuring out solutions, and planning next month's sales conference.

Upon arriving at the office, Sharon goes straight to her yoga class. As CEO, she is dedicated to creating a workplace that supports the whole person. One way she expresses this is by offering free yoga classes three times a day to all employees and their significant others. She chooses to practice twice a week at the office. After a shower, she is at her desk by 10 a.m. Years ago Sharon couldn't have imagined starting her official work day at 10 a.m. but she has learned that both the quality and the quantity of her work grow as she pays attention to radically taking care of herself.

Sharon has already identified her top three priorities for the day and set aside ninety minutes to focus on her most important work. Aware that she does her best mental work in the morning, she rarely schedules meetings or calls before noon. Members of her team know that she is accessible if they need her. Together they have developed agreements about what constitutes "needing" one another, virtually eliminating "drive-by interruptions" unless an emergency arises. They follow communication protocols for using texts, emails, voicemail, phone, video conference, and face-to-face meetings, matching the bandwidth of the medium with the significance of their communication needs. For example, meaningful conversations that include complex ideas and a full range of emotions are covered in person or on Skype. This commitment alone has stopped issues from recirculating through endless email chains.

Speaking of emotions, Sharon and her team have become experts at experiencing and expressing emotions in healthy ways that bring life, vibrancy, and great wisdom to each of them individually and to the group as a whole. As a result of this and many of their other practices, employee engagement is at an all-time high, turnover at an all-time low, and health care costs the lowest they have been in years.

Sharon meets with her team for lunch every day. This isn't an obligation (very little is done in Sharon's world from "shoulds" or "have tos"), but rather an opportunity few of them miss. The lunch is filled with laughter and play. It's not that they're playing ping-pong (though there is a ping-pong table in the corporate lounge) or telling silly jokes. They're actually having fun dealing with real business issues.

What is striking about Sharon and her team is the way this spirit of play permeates everything they do. One of their mottos is "Nothing is serious. If it seems serious, SHIFT." Now don't misunderstand this. Sharon and her team are wildly successful. They have lapped the field when it comes to all the metrics of individual and team success. Their investors couldn't be more pleased. It's just that Sharon learned (she would say, "the hard way") that taking yourself or life seriously leads to all kinds of physical, emotional, relational, and occupational "issues." Sharon is a deeply grounded person who has a real sense that her security is rooted in something way beyond performance. It just IS. She and her teammates have learned this through direct experience, for them it is not just a set of beliefs.

A good part of what makes work and lunch so much fun at Sharon's firm is the degree to which they value learning over everything else. To them, learning combined with playing is the holy grail of their corporate culture. They aren't that interested in being "right" or proving that they're right, knowing that this takes care of itself if they focus on staying in a state of curiosity and high learning. They all drift in and out of this state but they identify their drifts, don't blame or shame themselves or one another, and shift rapidly back to a high state of learning and collaboration. Drama, gossip, and toxic fear, rarely seen around the firm, are quickly addressed and resolved.

So much of the energy consumed in other companies through these and other forms of toxic sludge is freed up for high levels of creativity, innovation, and collaboration. No wonder the firm is regularly listed as one of the best places to work.

After lunch Sharon returns to her office and "processes" her email. She doesn't check her email constantly. In fact, all alarms to notify her of a new email have been turned off. Processing her email (viewing every message and doing the appropriate thing with it, which is often just filing it) takes about ninety minutes of Sharon's day. She usually does this in two sittings: right after lunch and again before leaving at the end of the day. Her teammates and clients understand that if they need to reach her, she will read and respond to emails within twenty-four hours. If they need a response before then, they know to contact Sharon's assistant or call Sharon directly. She does not live in the "tyranny of the urgent." She gave up that addiction long ago.

The afternoon includes meetings and one-on-one coaching, along with several walks around the building. Sharon has learned that she works best in sixty- to ninety-minute increments separated by ten minutes of walking or moving creatively. She honors this and other rhythms in her life.

Sharon has become an expert at leading a high performing executive team. First of all, she is vigilant about only having people on her team who live the culture. Second, she only works directly with people around whom her energy increases. She pays attention to this and if her energy starts to drop in the presence of one of her direct reports she has a candid and open conversation to address the issue. Third, she is a master delegator. She lives and works in her areas of "genius" and empowers everyone else to do the same. Accountability is so artfully practiced by Sharon and her team that she would never think of having people work for her that she has to "hold accountable." Everyone on the team gets that responsibility is something you take and not something that anyone else can assign to you. Her team takes responsibility for themselves, for the team and for the organization as a whole. With everyone working in their zone of genius, and no time wasted in drama, Sharon is able to get done in 7-8 hours of work what others could only imagine accomplishing in 24/7.

By 6:00 she is seated in the back of her car and usually spends another twenty minutes meditating. At home she connects with her husband and children for dinner, homework and reading together before bed. Like many leading executives, Sharon travels her fair share, and when she is home, she makes these moments count. Usually in bed by 10:00, she rests peacefully. Everything is okay, just as it is meant to be.

It's been another good day.

Sharon is a highly successful leader.

Sharon is a conscious leader.

This book is for all the Tims of the world who suspect that there is a better way of leading and living. This book is about conscious leadership.

Leading Above The Line
15 Commitments of conscious Leadership

LEADING FROM ABOVE THE LINE

Several times a year one of us is invited to speak to one of the top Wall Street investment banks. We present to the firm's top leaders and their key clients about conscious leadership. Like most investment banks, this is not exactly a bastion for new age, touchy-feely leadership experimentation. It is a hard-edged, competitive, no-nonsense, bottom-line-focused commercial enterprise. And we begin almost every session the same way—by drawing a single black line:

That's right. A black line. Then we step away and say to some of the world's top business leaders, "From our perspective, this diagram is the most important model we know of for being a conscious leader." Often this declaration is greeted with silence and skeptical looks. We're not surprised. These leaders work with complex models and sophisticated concepts, so a statement claiming that a simple black line is the best model for conscious leadership would understandably raise some eyebrows.

We go on to say that this model is binary: it is either/or. At any point, a leader is either above the line or below the line. If you are above it, you are leading consciously, and if you are below it, you are not.

We then ask all the participants where they currently are with respect to the line, explaining that conscious leaders know at any given moment whether they are above or below it. Frustration builds because these types of leaders like to "get it right." In fact, they get paid for getting it right and don't like to make mistakes, especially in public.

This exercise replicates real-world leadership. Leaders make decisions (am I above or below the line?). They make decisions with limited information (I don't know what the model means), and they judge those decisions as right or wrong. Their decisions are subject to public scrutiny, so the world judges them as well. This combination of factors usually leads to some amount of anxiety, and this anxiety is the water in which most leaders swim. Some swim in these waters consciously and others do it unconsciously.

After everyone has committed to being above or below the line by a show of hands, we go on to describe the model. We share with them that when leaders are below the line, they are closed and defensive, and when they are above the line, they are open and curious. Further, we reveal that when leaders are below the line, their primary commitment is to being right, and when they are above the line, their primary commitment is to learning.

After presenting this information, we ask again for a show of hands—who is above the line and who is below it? At this point, interesting leadership and social phenomena kick in. These smart, capable leaders have made a judgment that it is "better" to be above the line than

ABOVE THE LINE

OPEN   CURIOUS   COMMITTED TO LEARNING

BELOW THE LINE

CLOSED   DEFENSIVE   COMMITTED TO BEING RIGHT

below it. This belief causes them to distort reality so they can see themselves as above the line, the preferred state, even if they are not above the line.

Into this common distortion (wanting to be right), we offer this coaching. We suggest that the first mark of conscious leaders is self-awareness and the ability to tell themselves the truth. It matters far more that leaders can accurately determine whether they are above or below the line in any moment than where they actually are. Distortion and denial are cornerstone traits of unconscious leaders.

A NORMAL STATE

We then explain to the bank's leaders and their invited guests that being below the line is actually a normal state for many people. According to Dan Goleman in his 1995 book *Emotional Intelligence*, we are constantly scanning our environment looking for threats. To be precise, the amygdala, an almond shaped part of the limbic brain, is standing guard "something like an emotional sentinel, challenging every situation, every perception, with but one kind of question in mind, the most primitive: 'Is this something I hate? That hurts me? Something I fear, if so – if the moment at hand somehow draws a 'Yes' – the amygdala reacts instantaneously, like a neural tripwire, telegraphing a message of crisis to all parts of the brain." (Goleman, pg. 16) When the amygdala senses a threat, it sounds an alarm and our entire system prepares for survival. When our ancestors were confronted with a threat to their survival in the form of a wild animal, they fought, ran, stood still, or fell to the ground to play dead. Their reaction was usually the option with the greatest probability for survival, often with no real thought. It was simply an instinctual reaction. The amygdala was doing its job.

Like our ancestors, leaders are constantly scanning the horizon for threats. But today, those threats rarely endanger their physical survival. There aren't many saber-toothed tigers roaming the campuses of corporate America.

Nevertheless, leaders often have a difficult time telling the difference between a threat to the body's physical survival and an imagined threat to the ego or identity. For example, when our boss frowns at us while we're making a presentation, we interpret this as a threat to our survival, at least the survival of our ego. In a threatened state the brain fires off a chemical cocktail designed to support us in fighting, fleeing, freezing, or fainting. Put another way, when we perceive a threat to our sense of well-being, we go "below the line." We don't choose this at a conscious level. We just do it. We close down. We get defensive and double down on being RIGHT.

WHAT'S WRONG WITH BEING RIGHT

What does being right have to do with being below the line? Remember, for most leaders, survival is a matter of protecting the ego or identity or image. And the ego firmly believes that if it is not "right," it will not survive. Being wrong equates to being dead. This is especially true as the level of perceived threat rises. The higher the stakes—for example, we could lose our job or the love of a significant other or control of something we deem important—the more the ego will try to survive by being right.

We see this again and again in our work with leaders. When coaching them, we often use the tool of feedback. We gather lots of data from multiple sources and give leaders feedback about how they are seen in the world and about how they appear to be wired at a personality level. Leader after leader will interpret this direct feedback as a threat to their identity and go below the line. It is a natural reaction.

For this reason, we say that knowing when you are below the line is more important than being below the line. Leaders are in real trouble when they are below the line (closed, defensive, and committed to being right and keeping their ego alive) and think they are above it. This leadership blindness is rampant in the corporate world.

But once leaders develop self-awareness and locate themselves accurately below the line, they create the possibility for shifting, a master skill of conscious leaders. Shifting is moving from closed to open, from defensive to curious, from wanting to be right to wanting to learn, and from fighting for the survival of the individual ego to leading from a place of security and trust.

CHOOSING TO SHIFT

Of course, many leaders ask us this question: "Why is it so important to be above the line?" From our experience, and probably yours, creativity, innovation, and collaboration (all keys to high-level problem solving) occur best when we operate above the line. In fact, they don't occur at all below the line, where it is necessary to be if your physical well-being is threatened and you need to fight, flee, freeze, or faint. In such a situation, survival trumps high-level problem solving, creativity, and collaboration. Most leaders work in environments in which creative problem solving is necessary for winning, but this is available only when leaders lead from above the line.

Since the early 1900s, based on what is called the Yerkes-Dodson effect, scientists have known that increased arousal is correlated with increased performance on a task up to some point and then as arousal continues to increase, performance declines. This inverted U shaped curve has shown up in many studies since. In our model being below the line is a state of hyperarousal (increased heart rate, anxiety feeling, pupillary dilation, change in respiratory rate, increased blood adrenaline levels). In this state certain tasks, especially those that require creativity and collaboration, are more difficult. For simple tasks, the more you are aroused, the better you behave but most leaders we coach are not dealing with simple tasks. We also prefer to see people choosing to lead from above the line because those leaders experience sustainable happiness. Happiness, as it is measured and researched, is essential to long-term health, engagement, and success.

Numerous studies have correlated happiness with lower levels of stress and better physical health. A critical issue in the corporate world is the high cost of health care. One of the best remedies for that is cutting down on illnesses. Happy people get sick less. And people who lead from above the line are both healthier and happier.

Further, companies spend countless sums of money to measure and improve employee engagement. In our experience, "above the line" leaders are more engaged and create environments with much higher levels of engagement among their team members.

A ROAD MAP

This book is about "location, location, location," as they say in the world of real estate. In our work with countless leaders, we have learned that at any moment, they are living from either a "below the line" commitment or an "above the line" commitment. The following 15 Commitments of Conscious Leadership provides a road map to help you constantly determine where you are with respect to the line. Each commitment has an "above the line" version (the commitment of conscious leaders) and a "below the line" version (the commitment of unconscious leaders).

We use the word "commitment" throughout the book and it is important to clarify what we mean. Commitment is a statement of what is. From our perspective, you can know your commitments by your results, not by what you say your commitments are. We are all committed. We are all producing results. Conscious leaders own their commitments by owning their results.

Here is a simple illustration: We are all committed (the way we use this word) to weighing exactly what we weigh in this moment. How do we know this? Because this is what is. In our experience, most people would "say" that they are committed to weighing more or less than they weigh in this moment. The result—not our words—is the proof of a commitment. As we introduce you to the 15 Commitments of Conscious Leadership, we are suggesting that at any moment, you are living either from the "above the line" commitment or from the "below the line" commitment. The results occurring in your life provide the evidence of which one.

Our passion is in supporting leaders to tell themselves the truth in any given moment, to locate themselves as above or below the line, and then, if they are willing, to shift into higher states of leadership consciousness. We offer many shift moves that have had a profound effect on leaders and their organizations.

CONTENT VS. CONTEXT

As you begin your journey with us into conscious leadership it is important for you to know that we place our attention primarily on context and secondarily on content. From our perspective all of life is occurring as one big conversation. Sometimes this conversation is between individual people, sometimes it's between groups

> *For us, commitment is a statement of "what is." From our perspective, you can know your commitments by your results, not by what you say your commitments are. We are all committed. We are all producing results. Conscious leaders own their commitments by owning their results.*

and nations. Sometimes this conversation is between an individual and the universe and often this conversation occurs inside one person and it is between various parts of me.

All conversations have both content and context. Content answers the question, "What are we talking about?" Context answers the question, "How are we talking about the content?" Most leaders and people focus on the content of conversation. For instance, the production line is broken down, what do we do to get it going; we aren't innovating fast enough; our market share is shrinking; our daughter's grades are slipping; I want to go to Tuscany for vacation. All of this is content. It is "what" we are talking about.

Context answers the question "how" are we talking about the content. Or put another way, "From what consciousness are we having this conversation?" Based on what we have talked about so far, we would suggest that all conversations occur either from above the line or below the line. We can talk about the broken production line from above or below the line. We can talk about market share or our daughter's grades or a vacation from above or below the line. This is a context question. In our experience great leaders pay more attention to how conversations are occurring than to what is being talked about. In fact, a specific leadership question that we see conscious leaders bringing to every situation is "Where are we talking and listening from right now: above or below the line?"

For each of the 15 Commitments we offer different contexts from which any conversation can occur, a below the line context and an above the line context. If leaders pay attention to the context of every conversation, the content will resolve itself much more easefully, creatively and sustainably.

THE FOUR WAYS OF LEADING

The discussion of being above and below the line is part of a larger conversation. The larger conversation is about states of consciousness.

When we talk about our work, we are often asked, "What exactly is conscious leadership?" Let's begin by looking at the word "conscious." If you walk down Michigan Avenue in Chicago and say to the average passerby, "The CEO of XYZ Corporation is unconscious," a normal response would be, "Wow, that's serious. Did he fall and hit his head or did he have a stroke or heart attack? Is he in the hospital? Will he live?"

Most people associate the word "unconscious" with the state that results from a severe blow to the head, or as the dictionary defines it, "a dramatic alteration of one's mental state that involves a complete or near complete lack of responsiveness to people and other environmental stimuli."

This common definition is also quite useful in our discussion. Unconscious leaders have a "complete or near complete lack of responsiveness to people and other environmental stimuli." They do not really see what is happening around them. They are cut off from an authentic experience of people, themselves, and their lives.

We often describe unconscious leaders as reactive. They react from a "story" about the past or an imagined future, and their personality, ego, or mind takes over. They are not free to lead from creative impulse, nor are they tuned in to what the moment is requiring of them.

For example, many top leaders have tremendous drive, passion, and energy, which sometimes go hand in hand with what the workplace calls "anger issues." It doesn't take long for leaders open to coaching to see that when their anger is out of control, they go on autopilot. They literally can't see what is happening (blind rage). They live out this familiar pattern again and again.

The same holds true for leaders in the grip of unconscious fear. When fear is occurring in them, they can't see it, feel it, experience it, or release it. Here's a typical scenario: A leader receives a report about missing the earnings target, and fear kicks him into reactivity. The next thing

> *...conscious leaders experience what is here now and respond in the moment. They are not trapped in old patterns. They are free to lead and serve others, their organization, the world, and themselves.*

you know he has his direct reports seated around him in a conference room, and once again, he's having a conversation about fault and blame.

Recently we coached the CEO of a highly successful Fortune 200 company. He's being lauded as a bright new star on the leadership front. Yet he confided in us that his autopilot reactivity shows up when he goes to a bar, has several drinks, and starts chasing women. This unconscious leader has been stuck in the same pattern since college.

Unlike unconscious leaders who do not see, hear, or feel authentically and accurately, conscious leaders experience what is here now and respond in the moment. They are not trapped in old patterns. They are free to lead and serve others, their organization, the world, and themselves.

In our experience, conscious leaders are rare. Most people live life largely unconsciously in the habitual trance of their personality, their regret and anger about the past, and their hope, fear, and greed about the future. Let us be clear: We are not judging this way of living. We live this way quite often ourselves. In fact, we actually think that this is the "normal" (familiar) way of living and it has real benefits. We'll discuss those later but for now we simply want to point out that people can lead and live differently.

FOUR WAYS OF LEADING IN THE WORLD

To help us have this conversation, we want to introduce a second model. We have already introduced you to Above and Below the Line. Like that model and all others, this next one is fundamentally flawed because no model can accurately describe reality, particularly the reality of human consciousness. All models are de facto distortions of reality. Just as a restaurant's menu is not the same as its food but merely a pointer to something much more wonderful, so are models only pointers to something far more complex.

We originally heard about this model in a talk Michael Bernard Beckwith, founder of Agape International Spiritual Center, gave on life visioning. The model immediately resonated with us as a way to describe what we observe in our work with leaders. We have extrapolated from Beckwith's original model by adding our own concepts to his construct.

The model on the next page suggests that there are four ways of leading.

We want to clarify that these four ways of being in the world are states, not stages of development. Stages are progressive sequential eras in the life of a person or organization. For example, a person undergoes the stages of infancy, childhood, adolescence, and adulthood. States, on the other hand, are not sequential. We don't move in a developmental pattern from one state to another, but rather in an ongoing, irregular way. Think of the awake, dreaming, and non-dreaming sleep states. People move in and out of these states throughout the day and night. One is not better or more advanced than another.

FOUR WAYS OF LEADING

AS ME - LIFE IS ME

POSTURE:	At one with all
EXPERIENCE:	Peace, spaciousness
BELIEFS:	There is just oneness
	There are no problems, and no one to "solve" them
KEY QUESTION:	No more questions - just knowingness
BENEFITS:	Experience oneness & non-dualism
	Unlimited freedom & peace

ONENESS

TO ME - LIFE HAPPENS TO ME

POSTURE:	Victim
EXPERIENCE:	Blaming and complaining
BELIEFS:	There is a problem
	Someone is at fault
	Someone should fix this
KEY QUESTION:	Why me? Whose fault is this?
BENEFITS:	Experience separateness
	Defined identity, entertaining drama, supports empathy, adrenaline high

This is an important clarification for us because when we present this model to leaders, they often interpret it as stages of development and that is not the intention. Indeed, moving from To Me to By Me to Through Me and back to To Me can take a matter of hours or minutes.

Becoming aware of which state we are in at any moment is the first key to shifting. As mentioned earlier in our discussion of above and below the line, location is critical in this work. Where are you living and leading from

THROUGH ME - I COOPERATE WITH LIFE HAPPENING

POSTURE: Co-creator

EXPERIENCE: Allowing, flow, wonder and awe

BELIEFS: I am the source of all meaning. I experience things as perfect, whole and complete
Life handles all apparent "problems"

KEY QUESTION: What wants to happen through me?

BENEFITS: Non-attachment
Unlimited possibility, plenty of everything

SURRENDER

BY ME - I MAKE LIFE HAPPEN

POSTURE: Creator

EXPERIENCE: Appreciation

BELIEFS: Problems are here for me to learn from
I create the problem, so I can solve it

KEY QUESTION: What can I learn?
What do I want to create?

BENEFITS: Personal empowerment
Define your wants and desires

RESPONSIBILITY

now? This is a question conscious leaders ask themselves regularly and become masters at answering accurately. Only then do we have the real option to shift to another state of leadership if that is what we want and are fully willing to do.

THE "TO ME" WAY OF LEADING

The To Me state of consciousness is synonymous with being below the line. From our perspective, 95% of all leaders (and people) spend 98% of their time in that state. If I am in the To Me consciousness, I see myself "at the effect of," meaning that the cause of my condition is outside me. It is happening To Me. Whether I see the cause as another person, circumstance, or condition, I believe I'm being acted upon by external forces.

Leaders in To Me are "at the effect of" the markets, competitors, team members who "don't get it," suppliers, the weather, their own mood, their spouse, their children, their bank account, and their health, to name a few. They believe that these external realities are responsible for their unhappiness (if only my spouse weren't mean, I'd be happy); for their failures (if only my sales team would work harder, our top line would go up); and for their insecurities (if my board gave me a larger share of the company, I'd be secure).

This "at the effect of" way of seeing the world doesn't mean that leaders are always unhappy or upset. On the contrary, some are quite happy and successful, but the point is that they are pinning the cause of their well-being on external factors.

We call this To Me mindset "victim consciousness". In our experience, a significant difference exists between being a victim and having a victim consciousness. Most people would agree that children abused by alcoholic parents are victims. Thirty years later, if those same children, now adults, are still blaming their parents for their problems and suffering, they are living in a victim consciousness.

Victim consciousness is a choice. As we mentioned, from our experience, most people choose to live this way.

Those operating in the To Me victim consciousness are constantly looking to the past to assign blame for their current experience. They fault themselves, others, circumstances, or conditions for what is happening in their lives. Their thoughts and conversations are often dominated by "why" questions: "Why did this happen to me?" "Why don't they respect me?" "Why are we losing market share?" "Why are my kids failing in school?" They search for answers that assign responsibility for the cause.

To see an example of this, we need look no further than the cable news networks. Whether you watch CNN, FOX, or MSNBC, every conversation goes like this: "Something is wrong. Someone is to blame. And that someone is not us. It is them. And we are right, they are wrong." Of course, they don't all agree on the "someone" or "something" to blame, but their common experience is grounded in the reality that something is wrong and someone "out there" is responsible.

The gateway for moving from To Me to By Me is responsibility...

THE "BY ME" WAY OF LEADING

When leaders shift from below the line to above it, they move from the To Me to the By Me state—from living in victim consciousness to living in creator consciousness and from being "at the effect of" to "consciously creating with." Instead of believing that the cause of their experience is outside themselves, they believe that they are the cause of their experience.

To Me leaders think that the world should be a certain way, and if it isn't, something needs to be different. For example, it should be warm and sunny out and it's not, therefore the weather should be different. My children should obey me and when they don't, they should be different. My employees should "get it" and they don't, so they need to be different. Sometimes, however, the world is just the way they think it should be, although this is rare and fleeting for To Me leaders.

The By Me leader chooses to see that everything in the world is unfolding perfectly for their learning and development. Nothing has to be different. They see that what is happening is for them.

We suggest to leaders that life is like one big learning university, where we all enroll in classes that are perfectly designed to support our education. In these classes, we can either be "at the effect of" the teacher, the curriculum, and the other students or "consciously creating with."

To do the latter, a leader chooses curiosity and learning over defensiveness and being right (two cornerstones of the To Me consciousness). Instead of asking "Why is this happening to me?" the By Me leader asks questions like, "What can I learn from this?" "How is this situation 'for me'?" "How am I creating this and keeping this going?"

The gateway for moving from To Me to By Me is responsibility—actually, what we call radical responsibility: choosing to take responsibility for whatever is occurring in our lives, letting go of blaming anyone (ourselves, others, circumstances, or conditions), and opening through curiosity to learn all that life has to teach us. We'll say much more about this in Commitment 1.

THE "THROUGH ME" WAY OF LEADING

Central to both the To Me and By Me states of leadership is "me": I am at the center of the consciousness. This doesn't mean that I don't think about other people or issues or God or the future or the past. Rather, it means that my thoughts in these states are about how everything relates to me. Again, from our perspective, this is not a bad thing. It is just the way the mind/ego/identity functions. From these states of consciousness, we can't interact with the world in any other way.

The "me" in the To Me state is "at the effect of" people, circumstances, and conditions. It is disempowered, invested in being right, and therefore defensive. In contrast, the "me" in the By Me state is "consciously creating with" people, circumstances, and conditions. It is empowered, interested in learning, and therefore very curious.

In the Through Me state of leadership, the "me" starts to open to another. Curiosity begins to guide this leader to a different set of questions, such as, "Am I the center of the universe?" "Is there something going on in addition to me?" "What is the nature of this other?" "Is it possible to be in relationship to this other?"

Let us be clear that in our experience, leaders who ask these questions are not necessarily religious, though sometimes they are. We work with scientists who ask these same questions and conclude that the "other" is the energy of the quantum field. Some leaders experience this entity as love or the universe or presence or God. The key to Through Me is that leaders begin to notice something beyond themselves.

We'll illustrate this with the subject of purpose or vision. To Me leaders rarely have a clearly aligned purpose or vision for themselves or their organization. They might have gone though an HR exercise and created a purpose, mission, and vision, but in their daily experience, they are not living from or for this purpose. This is actually part of the reactive pattern that defines the To Me victim consciousness.

When leaders move through the gateway of responsibility into the consciousness of By Me, they become very committed and aligned with their purpose. They first get clear about their individual purpose and then create organizational purpose. At any moment, By Me leaders are either on purpose or off it and if the latter occurs, they shift and get back on purpose. They come to their purpose by asking the question, "What do I want?" Often we coach them to ask the second, deeper question, "What do I really want?" By Me leaders sit with this question until they have an answer, and then they align themselves with this purpose. This purpose can and often does change, but By Me leaders are clear about their purpose.

For more on Through Me Purpose listen to the audio series on Sounds True by Michael Bernard Beckwith on "Life Visioning."

As leaders open up to Through Me, their purpose question changes. They ask, "What is life's highest idea of itself that wants to manifest in and through me?" The word "life" could be love or God or the universe or presence or the quantum field.

To most people, this question sounds weird at first but as Through Me leaders sit in it, they have a very different experience than their By Me counterparts. Through Me leaders do not try to "figure out" their answer, which would be By Me consciousness. Instead, they listen attentively to what wants to be communicated to them. They understand that there is another moving in the world that wants to make something happen in and through them.

When leaders follow this practice, we tell them that the communication can manifest in various ways. Some leaders get a sense of words, others experience pictures, sounds or colors, while still others receive just an intuitive impression. What we know is that if leaders are fully willing, the communication occurs reliably. This practice can be used not only by individual leaders but also by entire teams.

The Greenville Health System in Greenville, South Carolina, is one of the largest health systems in the Southeast. CEO Mike Riordan is committed to conscious leadership. He understands all four of these ways of being in the world and knows that he moves in and out of them with regularity and dexterity.

A few years ago, Mike and the senior leaders of GHS were on a retreat and decided to do Through Me visioning. They asked this question: "What is health care's biggest idea of itself that wants to manifest in and through GHS?" They listened with expectancy, knowing that something bigger than themselves was wanting to do something at their organization. Over time (and this is often the case), they collectively got an understanding that what wanted to happen through them was a transformation of health care. Since then, the top leaders of the health system have been living and leading from this vision. They have gotten very clear about what it means for them to transform health care and they are taking the steps to make it happen. One powerful example: they decided that to transform healthcare, they had to transform the consciousness of physicians. They had to change the way doctors were trained, and to do that, they realized they had to start a medical school. This is no small thing. Rarely do new medical schools begin. In September 2012, GHS welcomed its first class of medical students into a new consciousness of medicine. Wow, this is Through Me leadership.

Just as responsibility is the gateway to move from To Me to By Me, surrender, or letting go, is the gateway to move from By Me to Through Me. For most leaders, this means letting go of control. When we first meet leaders, almost all have a strong control plan, where their ego is invested in the appearance of control. In truth, very little is under our control, but the To Me and By Me leaders believe the contrary.

The letting go of control—or more specifically, letting go of wanting to be in control of people, things, and circumstances we were never meant to be in control of and have never really been in control of—is powerful and often chaotic. We haven't met many people who surrender easily, casually, or comfortably. Most experience ongoing struggles and resistance. Letting go is an action that is taken again and again.

The paradox in leadership is that when we are in To Me, we experience very little control because we are "at the effect of" what is happening in our lives. Part of the fun of By Me leadership is that we experience a sense of control and power. It is the power of being in a place of responsibility, creativity, and ownership. It's exhilarating. Then leaders are asked to surrender, and often their response is, "What? I finally got a sense of empowerment and control and now you [life, love, God] are asking me to surrender." Yes, this is what life asks of all of us. Surrender for the Through Me leader is not optional.

THE "AS ME" WAY OF LEADING

The fourth state of leadership is As Me, the level of consciousness we speak least about because most leaders are not ready or interested in the discussion and experience. We respect that. At the same time, we would like to offer a few words about As Me consciousness to complete the model.

As Me consciousness has two aspects. The first is oneness. Most of the great religions, philosophies, and spiritual teachings have an understanding of oneness, the experience that there is no separation—there is only one reality and it is not divided. Sometimes, this is called non-duality, which simply means "not two." Again, scientists give words to this when they say that energy is all there is and it is not divisible. What appears hard and solid to the senses is actually not so hard and solid. If we magnified everything under the most powerful microscope, we would discover that what appears solid is actually only space. We would also discover that boundaries of separation that appear solid (the boundary between your arm and the table on which it rests, or between you and me) are not solid at all.

As Me leaders realize this oneness. It is not simply a philosophy or belief for them. It is a direct experience. Once a leader discovers the truth of what is—oneness— and who they are, their consciousness shifts dramatically. Just as a thought experiment, imagine for a moment how you would lead and live in a world without separation; no separation between you and your employees or you and your competitors or you and the environment. From our experience, everything looks radically different from this consciousness.

The second aspect of As Me is the absence of a personal "me." Not only is everyone and everything one—there is no separation—and also no personal center. As one of our teachers Hale Dwoskin says, "In the As Me space, there are no problems and there is no you to have a problem." In To Me and By Me, the "me" is central. In Through Me, the "me" begins to recede in surrender to the other, and in As Me, "me" doesn't exist at all.

One way we teach this Four Ways of Being Model is by looking at the questions asked in each state of consciousness. We have covered some of the questions for the first three. The As Me state is unique because it has no questions. The full realization of As Me is the experience of no more questions, no seeking, no suffering. This doesn't mean that you wouldn't ask a question like, "How do I improve throughput in our plant?" What it

THE FOUR WAYS OF BEING MODEL

	TO ME RESPONSIBILITY	**BY ME** SURRENDER
MONEY	▸ Scarcity = Never enough ▸ I work hard to get it ▸ My value is attached to it	▸ I want more ▸ I can create more ▸ It is a measure of my value
TIME	▸ There is not the right amount ▸ I am stressed because of it ▸ I am overwhelmed, busy/bored	▸ I'm in control of my time ▸ I use time management systems ▸ I use it to do what I want
HAPPINESS	▸ It is a fleeting moment of pleasure (ice cream, vacation, sex) ▸ It depends on circumstances	▸ I choose to make myself happy ▸ I make happiness if I bring the right ingredients
DISCIPLINE	▸ Always too much or too little ▸ It's hard; I "should"; "I have to" ▸ It is necessary to be good	▸ I choose it (to delay gratification) ▸ I use it as a tool to create
PURPOSE	▸ What purpose? ▸ I should have one and don't ▸ I just have roles I play	▸ My purpose ▸ I declare it and go out and get it ▸ Both takes energy and energizing
LEADERSHIP	▸ It's a role; I have it or I don't ▸ It comes with have-tos, burden and incompetent followers	▸ There are skills/techniques to master which create good or effective leadership

THROUGH ME ONENESS ➤	AS ME

THROUGH ME ONENESS ➤   **AS ME**

- It is abundant
- It is an energy not a thing
- Measurement is irrelevant

- It is just another form
- It is given and received with freedom and joy

- I have plenty of it
- There is only now - there is no past or future

- I am the source of it
- It is an illusion - like all other illusions

- It is here now
- It has a deep lasting quality
- I relax into joy

- Happiness is just another state, it is just one of many vibrations passing through

- It is effortless
- Having and delaying gratification are equals

- Can you find the one who is disciplined?

- Transcendent purpose
- No more wanting
- I receive it through listening

- What purpose? Being and purpose are the same
- Impossible to be off of it

- It arises in response to present need; no "one" is the leader in co-creation

- There is no one to lead and nowhere to lead to

means is that all questions about purpose, identity, life, and so on, are replaced by the constant experience of life in the moment. When we say that there is no more suffering, we don't mean that pain, sadness, anger, and fear disappear, or that disease and death no longer occur. But in As Me, there is no suffering in the presence of these and all experiences.

For those of you who are particularly curious about Though Me and As Me states we offer some of our favorite tools for this exploration in the resource section at the end of the book.

From our experience most leaders are well served by focusing on the shift from To Me to By Me. While we value all four states of consciousness, this book is about moving from To Me to By Me. We place our attention on this movement, and suggest you do as well, because at this point we don't know of an entire organization that is living from By Me on a consistent basis.

HOW TO USE THIS BOOK

We highly recommend that you read and master the first two commitments before moving on to the others. Becoming skilled in responsibility and curiosity are essential to shifting from To Me to By Me, and they create a context that will support you in exploring and practicing the other thirteen and integrating them into your daily life.

With this foundation in place, proceed to Commitment 3, emotional intelligence. Proficiency in the world of feelings is critical to understanding and implementing all the other commitments.

Then continue on to Commitments 4–9, in whatever order you choose. These six commitments describe ways of being in the world. Conscious leaders have the awareness and determination to turn their beliefs into behaviors. For instance, it is easy to believe in eating a healthy diet, but turning that into action requires commitment. The behaviors of candor (#4), eliminating gossip (#5), integrity (#6), appreciation (#7), living in our genius (#8), and play (#9) differentiate conscious and unconscious leaders.

Next, Commitments 10–12 present the worldviews underlying the behaviors of conscious leadership. Some may consider them radical. They include recognizing that the opposite of the beliefs you cling to so tightly could be as true as your beliefs (#10) and that nothing outside you can give you what you most long for—in fact, nothing can give it to you, because you already have it (#11) and you will always have enough (#12).

Commitments 13 and 14 suggest a new way of being in relationship—whether with a partner, a team, an organization, a community, or the world—that supports everyone having different interests and perspectives. Commitment 15 pays homage to Gandhi and other wise revolutionaries who have espoused that we be the solution we want to see in the world.

Each chapter has specific practices to help you embody the commitment. We strongly recommend that you spend time in daily practice. Find a learning partner (or several) so you can encourage each other to live as consciously as possible.

From our perspective this book is both a book to be read and a set of practices to be implemented. Let us be clear. If you think you can read this book and become a conscious leader without practicing you're kidding yourself. This is an ongoing process. The three of us have been practicing all the commitments for many years and we are still learning something new about conscious leadership nearly every day.

We urge you to avoid making this work too hard or taking it too seriously. Enjoy the journey as much as you can. Remember to play and laugh.

Leading from Above the Line

► Leadership operates from one of two places: above the line or below the line.

► Above the line leadership is open, curious, and committed to learning.

► Below the line leadership is closed, defensive, and committed to being right.

► Leading from below the line is not wrong— it is a common state.

► As a regular practice, conscious leaders notice when they are below the line and choose to shift to above the line.

► The Four Ways of Leading model shows the states of consciousness leaders operate in: To Me, By Me, Through Me, and As Me.

► Leaders are well served by focusing first on the shift from To Me to By Me leadership.

COMMITMENT ONE
Taking Radical Responsibility

I commit to taking full responsibility for the
circumstances of my life and for my physical,
emotional, mental, and spiritual well-being.
I commit to supporting others to take full
responsibility for their lives.

*I commit to blaming others and myself for
what is wrong in the world. I commit to being
a victim, villain, or a hero and taking more
or less than 100% responsibility.*

Blame is a powerful motivator. Like its cousins guilt and
shame, it is one of the most common forms of motivation
used by leaders, parents, politicians, and clergy.

A typical executive team meeting at almost any
corporation illustrates this truth.

It's the Tuesday morning Executive Team meeting at
"Common Corp." Today happens to be the first meeting
after the quarter close, and the numbers don't look good.

The VP of sales begins by defending why his numbers
came in below forecast. "I'll cut to the chase," he says.

"Manufacturing didn't meet the deadline. The customer got upset and cancelled the order. I did everything I could to keep them in the deal, but they said they've had it with us missing scheduled deliveries."

To which the VP of manufacturing retorts, "I told all of you that the timelines we committed to were unrealistic and asked the sales team to renegotiate, but they said it was a deal killer to do that. Add the fact that our vendor screwed up and sent us the wrong parts for two of the projects, and we didn't stand a chance. I'm tired of trying to live up to the sales team's unrealistic delivery dates."

Back to the VP of sales. "And I'm tired of my teammates killing themselves to get business and then having manufacturing fail again and again to deliver quality products on time."

At this point, the president steps in. "Here's the bottom line," she says. "You're both to blame, and if you can't work out your differences, I'll find somebody who can. You both know how important the team is to me, and right now neither of you is a good teammate."

With blood pressures rising, and anger and defensiveness seeping out of everyone's pores, the VP of HR speaks up. "Now calm down everyone. Anger won't help us resolve the issues. We all know the economy stinks, and we're fighting serious head winds. I think the core problem has to do with communication. We're just not listening to each other, and I blame myself for that. I've had a communication effectiveness course on my to-do list for over six months, and I just haven't gotten to it because of the union negotiations."

On and on the conversation goes. We've all taken part in these blame fests, whether at work or at home. When things don't go the way we want them to go—when milk gets spilled at the dinner table, or Johnny flunks math, or Suzy gets a DUI, or the credit cards get overcharged—the default setting for most of us is to place blame and find fault. Depending on how people are wired, they blame either someone else, themselves, or the system. The system is the meta-problem or cause, like the economy, the Republicans, ObamaCare, God, or karma.

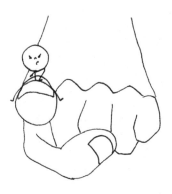

WHY WE BLAME

Blame, shame, and guilt all come from the same source: TOXIC FEAR. When things don't go the way we think they should (whether it be spilled milk or missing our quarterly numbers), the natural human reaction is to become anxious. Once fear kicks in, a common defense mechanism is to blame someone, something, or ourselves so we can keep our sense of identity (our ego) intact.

The pattern is simple and predictable:

1. Something doesn't go the way we think it should.

2. We become stuck in fear (often the anger that we feel is masking our fear).

3. We blame others, ourselves, or the system.

4. Relationships solidify around the roles of victim, villain, and hero.

Let's look at the relationship dynamic that supports a fear-based, blame-shame-guilt interaction.

Victims see themselves as "at the effect of." "It" is being done "to them" by someone or something out of their control. Typically they complain, either overtly or covertly, subtly or loudly, that "this isn't fair." Underneath all their words and actions is a tone of whining.

Villains find fault and place blame. Sometimes they point the finger at a person, at themselves, or at the meta-cause, but they deal with fear by looking for who's to blame.

Heroes hate conflict, pain, and tension and seek to temporarily relieve their discomfort without really dealing with the issue. They habitually over function and take more than their share of responsibility. A good number of the leaders we coach have made successful careers out of behaving in this way. In fact, heroes in many organizations are promoted, compensated, and enshrined as examples of doing "what it takes" to get the job done. Yet we believe that heroing is a primary form of unconscious leadership. It is toxic because it leads to burn out, supports others in taking less than their full responsibility (being victims), and rewards behaviors that ultimately lead to individual and team breakdown.

Heroes hate conflict, pain, and tension and seek to temporarily relieve their discomfort without really dealing with the issue.

At Common Corp, the leaders of sales and manufacturing, as well as the president, were all playing both victim and villain. The VP of sales was "at the effect of" (victim) manufacturing and the customer and blamed (villain) manufacturing. The VP of manufacturing was "at the effect of" an unrealistic deadline and a vendor who didn't deliver the right parts and blamed the sales team. The president was "at the effect of" her team and blamed her colleagues for not being better teammates.

The HR lead stepped into the fray as the hero. Clearly not liking the tension and anger, he wanted everyone to calm down. He wanted the conflict to go away without really addressing the issue. He added a bit of villain when he blamed himself. Some villains prefer that to blaming others.

Toxic fear drives the victim-villain-hero triangle. Blame, shame, and guilt keep it going. As we said at the beginning, blame and its root cause—toxic fear—are powerful motivators. But they also leave a negative residue: resentment and bitterness, along with low learning states, demotivation, and eventual demoralization. These toxic residues lead to high turnover and low innovation, creativity, and collaboration. No team can win with these elements corroding their effectiveness long term.

We have observed that leaders typically use five levels of motivation:

1. Toxic fear: blame, shame, and guilt
2. Extrinsic motivation: money, title, the corner office, and other perks
3. Intrinsic motivation: learning, fulfilling purpose, and autonomy
4. Play, creativity, and expressing our "genius" in the world
5. Love

Levels one and two always leave a negative residue, whereas levels three through five don't. Great leaders learn to motivate using methods that don't leave a negative residue, so they lead from levels three through five.

TAKING RESPONSIBILITY

The opposite of blaming is taking responsibility. The cornerstone commitment of leaders who move from To Me leadership to By Me leadership is Commitment 1:

I commit to taking full responsibility for the circumstances of my life and for my physical, emotional, mental, and spiritual well-being. I commit to supporting others to take full responsibility for their lives.

In our experience, Commitment 1 is radical. The word radical can mean "root or fundamental" as well as "extreme." In this case, Commitment 1 is both fundamental and extreme. It is fundamental because without it, leaders don't live the other fourteen commitments and never get out of the "To Me" box. It is extreme because it is so counter to the way people normally lead and live.

The key phrase is "taking full responsibility"—as opposed to "placing blame." "Placing" is moving something away from ourselves, and "taking" is moving something toward ourselves. Psychologists refer to this as the "locus of control." When we place blame, we locate the cause and control of our lives outside ourselves. When we take responsibility, we locate the cause and control of our lives inside ourselves.

Victims and villains locate the cause outside themselves, just as they did at Common Corp. Things didn't go the way they thought they should and the cause was something outside themselves: other departments, vendors, the team, the economy, or unions.

In our experience, taking full responsibility is based on a fundamental belief, and this, too, is radical.

Most people believe that there is a way the world should be and a way the world shouldn't be. In fact, we would assert that this is the most common belief among human beings. Of course there are great differences between the way people hold that belief (for example, Republicans versus Democrats), but they all hold their beliefs as right.

As long as we believe that there is a way the world should be (e.g. we should meet our quarterly targets) and a way the world shouldn't be (e.g. milk shouldn't be spilled), life won't work according to our beliefs. Simply put, life won't always turn out the way we think it should. And when that happens, we typically react by becoming anxious, resentful, or controlling and try to force the world to fit our beliefs. One primary means of doing this is placing blame on others, ourselves, or circumstances. We place the locus of control outside ourselves and say life isn't turning out the way it should because "they" messed up.

The alternative is to say, "I [We] messed up," and though some think this is taking responsibility, it is still based in blame and leaves a negative residue. In fact, often when we start working with leaders, they understand rather quickly that blaming others is poor leadership. But since they still believe that the world isn't the way it should be, they resort to blaming themselves and end up modeling self-blame for others. We want to be very clear: self-blame is equally as toxic as blaming others, or circumstances, and it is NOT taking responsibility.

But do a thought experiment with us. What if there is no way the world should be and no way the world shouldn't be? What if the world just shows up the way the world shows up? What if the great opportunity of life isn't in trying to get the world to be a certain way, but rather in learning from whatever the world gives us? What if curiosity and learning are really the big game, not being right about how things should be? Can you see how this would radically change the way we see and live our lives?

What if the big questions of life were not "How can we fix this?" or "How can we keep this from happening?" or "Who's to blame for this being this way?" but instead "What can we learn from this since life is all about learning and growing?" Or "Hmm… I wonder what this is here to teach me about myself and life?"

So the first step in taking responsibility is to shift from believing that the world should be a particular way to believing that the world just shows up. Second, we need to shift from rigidity, close-mindedness, and self-righteousness to curiosity, learning, and wonder (which naturally occurs once our beliefs change). All drama in leadership and life is caused by the need to be right. Letting go of that need is a radical shift all great leaders make.

In our experience, we can boost this shift by taking a third step. So far we're just suggesting that the world shows up the way the world shows up—it's indifferent about outcomes. But what if the world/universe/God/ Supreme Reality isn't just benign or agnostic? What if it is actually for us? What if, as Einstein wondered, the world is beyond benign to the point of actually being benevolent? Then what happens is not just a neutral experience, but rather a custom-ordered curriculum for our highest development as people and as members of teams and organizations. Although this third step isn't necessary for taking full responsibility, it does supercharge the shift. From this perspective, we can feel gratitude for whatever is occurring in our lives, greasing the wheels of learning, curiosity, and wonder.

ENCOURAGING OTHERS
TO BE RESPONSIBLE

The second part of Commitment 1 is "I commit to supporting others to take full responsibility for their lives." We've found that the key to making this happen is to take full responsibility for our own lives. When we move away from blaming, criticizing, and living in victim-villain-hero mode, we naturally invite others to do the same—without even saying a word. Step two in supporting others is to form relationships at work and home where all parties make a conscious decision to end blame and criticism and to take 100% responsibility for their lives, committing to learning and curiosity versus being right.

COMMITMENT IN ACTION

If you want to see a place where they are learning about taking 100% responsibility, visit Athletico, a premier provider of physical and occupational therapy as well as fitness services. Located in the Midwest, Athletico has over 70 locations and 1,000 team members. Five years ago, the top leadership of the organization, under the guidance of CEO Mark Kaufman, made a commitment to end blame and criticism. They are creating a culture that values learning over being right and taking 100% responsibility.

Now when situations arise (formerly known as problems, crises, and issues), the standard response of the leadership of Athletico is "Hmm... this is interesting, what can we learn from this?" A second common response is "I want to take my 100% responsibility and see how I helped create this situation. I want to get all my learnings."

During a recent coaching conversation, Mark brought up a situation with a manager who wasn't meeting her performance goals. As we explored it, Mark's very first line of inquiry was, "What can I learn about this and about my leadership of the organization?" When he wondered about this, he realized that he had not followed his instincts in dealing with this manager, failing to speak candidly with her about his thoughts and concerns. He had avoided conflict and withheld himself, thereby cocreating the situation. When Mark spoke to the manager, he began by sharing what he'd learned and taking full responsibility for what was occurring. He invited her to do the same. There was no blame, shame, or guilt. They both stayed in a high state of learning and curiosity.

Life and leadership don't always go this way at Athletico. Like almost all of us, they "drift" off their commitment to taking responsibility. They slide into blame, criticism, and defensiveness, and wanting to be right. But because the leaders have made a collective commitment to honor Commitment 1, they practice shifting out of blame and into learning. They know how to move away from the victim-villain-hero triangle and into greater co-creativity.

PRACTICING THE COMMITMENT

One tool they use at Athletico, and one that we see many leaders using, is the following Taking 100% Responsibility Worksheet.

TAKING 100% RESPONSIBILITY PROCESS

STEP 1: Identify an issue/complaint about anything going on in your life. State the complaint in "unenlightened" terms. Be dramatic. Ham it up. Blame overtly.

STEP 2: Step into 100% responsibility. Physically find a place in the room that represents your internal shift to being 100% responsible for the situation.

STEP 3: Gain insight by completing these statements, repeating each of them several times, until you have what feels like a breakthrough:

- *From the past this reminds me of...*
- *I keep this issue going by...*
- *What I get from keeping this issue going is...*
- *The lifelong pattern I'm noticing is...*
- *I can demonstrate 100% responsibility concerning this issue by...*

STEP 4: If during Step 3, you do not experience a shift, go back to Step 1 and repeat the process.

DEVELOPED BY HENDRICKS.COM

LISTENING TO
YOUR QUESTIONS

Finally, we have learned that you can tell what kind of a leader you are and what kind of a culture you are creating by paying attention to the kinds of questions you ask.

In blame cultures, where people take more or less than 100% responsibility, we hear leaders and everyone else ask these questions:

- *Who did it?*
- *Why did it happen?*
- *What is the root cause?*
- *Who participated in the chain of events that led to this?*
- *Who dropped the ball?*
- *Who's going to fix it?*

On the other hand, in curiosity/learning cultures, where people take 100% responsibility, leaders and others ask these questions:

- *Am I willing to take full responsibility for this situation?*
- *What do I really want?*
- *If there were no obstacles, what would I be doing with my creative energy?*
- *Am I willing to learn whatever it is I most need to learn about this situation?*
- *Am I willing to see all others involved as my allies?*
- *Am I willing to see myself as empowered in this situation?*
- *How can I play with this situation?*
- *Where and when do I feel most alive?*
- *What am I distracting myself from doing or knowing?*

IN A NUTSHELL

From our experience, making the choice to take full responsibility is the foundation of true personal and relational transformation. The entire game changes when we choose to see that we're creating our experience, and that someone or something is NOT doing it TO US.

Taking Radical Responsibility

- ▶ Taking full responsibility for one's circumstances (physically, emotionally, mentally, and spiritually) is the foundation of true personal and relational transformation.

- ▶ Blame, shame, and guilt all come from toxic fear.

- ▶ Toxic fear drives the victim-villain-hero triangle, which keeps leaders and teams below the line.

- ▶ This leads to high employee turnover and low innovation, creativity, and collaboration.

- ▶ Conscious leaders and teams take full responsibility—radical responsibility— instead of placing blame.

- ▶ Radical responsibility means locating the cause and control of our lives in ourselves, not in external events.

- ▶ Instead of asking "Who's to blame?", conscious leaders ask, "What can we learn and how can we grow from this?"

- ▶ Conscious leaders are open to the possibility that instead of controlling and changing the world, perhaps the world is just right the way it is. This creates huge growth opportunities on a personal and organizational level.

COMMITMENT TWO

Learning Through Curiosity

I commit to growing in self-awareness.
I commit to regarding every interaction
as an opportunity to learn. I commit to
curiosity as a path to rapid learning.

*I commit to being right and to seeing this
situation as something that is happening to
me. I commit to being defensive, especially
when I am certain that I am RIGHT.*

Current research on leadership shows that over the course
of our career, four competencies trump all others as the
greatest predictors of sustained success: self-awareness,
learning agility, communication, and influence. The
last two deal with how leaders interact with their world,
and the first two address leaders' internal relationship
to "reality." Self-awareness and learning agility are what
Commitment 2 of Conscious Leadership is all about.

Several times a year we hold The Conscious Leadership
Group Foundation retreats to introduce successful leaders
to the 15 Commitments of Conscious Leadership. Many
who attend have outstanding professional pedigrees, but
none better than Sarah, a recent participant. A graduate
from Yale with an MBA from Harvard, Sarah was a

competitive collegiate athlete. She went on to found a very successful company that Fortune magazine listed as one of the best technology start-ups of the decade. When we met her, she had just sold her share of the business and was looking for her next professional adventure. To say the least, Sarah is extremely bright, highly motivated, and uniquely skilled.

But Sarah wasn't curious or interested in self-awareness. This combination of superior executive skills and deficient self-awareness is not uncommon. We see it in our work all the time and recognized it in Sarah at the very beginning of the retreat. We also picked up on her defensiveness, which started out mild and grew in intensity until she was seething with anger. Many of the processes we do at The Conscious Leadership Group Foundation retreats involve giving and receiving feedback. Most of the leaders who attend have risen to the place in their career where they are isolated from direct feedback, so for many, hearing it from their peers is a new experience—as it was for Sarah.

Some of the early feedback Sarah received concerned her lack of congruity, meaning that she was giving off very mixed messages: saying one thing with her words, but something entirely different with her posture, facial expression, and tone of voice. At first, she responded to the comments with a laid-back attitude, looking detached and impenetrable (a common posture for leaders in a new environment in which they do not perceive themselves to be in control). When offered observations from the group about her lack of openness and curiosity, Sarah simply brushed them aside. But as the day wore on, she became more passive-aggressive and at one point suggested that it would be more beneficial for her to just go for a walk. When the group invited her to honor that preference and come back when she was willing to participate, she chose to leave for the afternoon.

When Sarah returned the next day, she demonstrated even less interest in self-awareness and curiosity. She received specific feedback about integrity glitches in her life, areas where she was not fully telling the truth and keeping her agreements. She first criticized the leaders and then the group as a whole. Her behavior culminated in her being asked to leave the retreat. Once she left, the entire group breathed a collective sigh of relief. They recognized that Sarah's defensiveness was consuming huge amounts of group energy and was no longer supporting their learning and growth. (By the way, this often happens in organizations: a leader's defensiveness hijacks group energy, bringing down the entire collaborative effort.)

Sarah was incredibly successful and will probably be successful again in her next venture. Also, she's still relatively young, so she will likely have the opportunity. In our experience, though, her style of relating to feedback does not sustain long-term success. Almost certainly, her defensiveness and lack of curiosity will catch up with her. Like many unconscious leaders, Sarah was far more interested in being RIGHT about her view of reality than in learning and growing.

i'm right... I'M RIGHT!

STUCK ON BEING RIGHT

I commit to being right and to seeing this situation as something that is happening to me. I commit to being defensive, especially when I am certain that I am RIGHT.

Quite possibly, no other commitment is more central to the core of unconscious people than the one to being right. This is for good reason. As we said in the introduction to the book, being right is connected to survival and survival is all that matters. Our brains are hardwired for self-preservation— we are constantly seeking to protect not only our physical well-being but our ego as well.

Please understand, the issue isn't "being right" but rather "wanting to be right" and "fighting to be right" and "proving we are right." When talking to a group, we often illustrate this by asking everyone to think of a simple, unarguable arithmetic axiom that they're confident is "right." Once this comes to their mind, we ask them to observe how "attached" they are to being right about this rule. How much energy do they have to fight for or defend the fact that 2 + 2 = 4 (the arithmetic axiom most people think of)? Usually they observe that they have very little energy to fight for the rightness of their belief. Why? From our perspective, it's because they know they are right and don't need to defend this law as though their identity or ego depended on it.

Next, we ask the same leaders to bring to mind an "issue" that they are fighting to be right about at work or in their private lives. It doesn't take them long to find one. When we invite them to notice the difference between their need to defend, justify, and explain why they are right about this issue and their need to defend $2 + 2 = 4$, they often have an epiphany.

Usually they discover two things. First, if they are honest with themselves, they see that they aren't nearly as certain about the "rightness" of their viewpoint as they act. Second, they realize that wanting to be right, being seen as being right, and being validated and appreciated for being right are what they really want. This attachment is all about the ego. What is "right" doesn't need to be defended. The equation $2 + 2 = 4$ doesn't require us to fight about its validity.

ABOVE AND BELOW THE LINE REVISITED

As we mentioned in the introduction to this book, one of our favorite models is this one:

Yes, it is only a line. But it has a profound meaning in this conversation. In our experience, at any point in time, we are either ABOVE the line or BELOW it. When we are

BELOW THE LINE

CLOSED   DEFENSIVE   COMMITTED TO BEING RIGHT

defensive, closed, and committed to being right, we are below the line. Or put another way, we are committed to the survival of our ego.

When we're open, curious, and committed to learning, we're above the line.

The grip of toxic fear drives behaviors and beliefs below the line. Presence brings forth behaviors and beliefs above the line. Below the line is a "To Me" experience, whereas above the line is a "By Me" experience. When we go below the line, the ego is fighting for survival and we become firmly entrenched in the scarcity belief: that there isn't enough—not enough love, time, money, energy, security, control, and approval. Above the line is opening to the big fun game of learning and growing, and we trust ourselves or Source (people have many different words for source like God, Allah, Universe, Presence, Love, Jesus, the Tao) to provide us with plenty of love, time, money, energy, security, control, and approval.

In our experience, conscious leaders choose to spend a lot of time above the line in high learning states. This "learning agility," mentioned in the beginning of the chapter, gives them a competitive advantage, since most people today are knowledge workers. In contrast, unconscious leaders spend too much time trying to be right, defending their ego, and being defensive, thereby diminishing their edge in the marketplace.

SHIFTING

This is not to say that conscious leaders don't go below the line and get defensive, closed, and invested in being right. They do. Remember, this response is hardwired into our survival instinct. But, contrary to unconscious leaders, conscious leaders regularly interrupt this natural reactivity. That means they take a moment to pause, breathe (literally take a conscious breath), and ask themselves this important question: "Where am I—above or below the line?" They're committed to self-awareness, so they answer it honestly. If they recognize that they've become reactive and are below the line, they don't shame or blame themselves or others. Actually, the first thing they do is accept themselves for being there. One breath of acceptance for what is true is essential. In fact, awareness and acceptance are the first two steps of all transformation.

One of our favorite models is the "Drift/Shift" model. We love it because it so represents our experience and the experience of many leaders. At the top of the model is presence. Presence is the state of being here… now in a non-reactive, non-triggered way. When a leader is present they are totally available to the moment and to what the moment is bringing to them. In presence they can be with what is occurring without being distracted by their personality, drama, anxiety, blame or beliefs about scarcity. In presence a leader can be with others, really be with others. They can listen, empathize, confront and create. In presence a leader can innovate, improvise and respond from their highest self, their genius. When two people in a relationship are in presence they can co-create, play and problem solve with incredible dexterity. Presence is the space from which intimate partners can really experience connection and intimacy.

THE DRIFT SHIFT MODEL

DEVELOPED BY HENDRICKS.COM

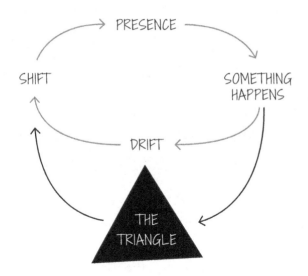

Presence can be called many things. It is called being in the flow or being in the zone. Athletes, artists and musicians all know what it is to be in presence. And so do great leaders. Our mentor Gay Hendricks, PhD says that most people currently stay in presence for about 4 seconds. At that point "Something Happens."

We love this phrase "something happens" because it is so benign. The something can be that a car cuts us off on the freeway, or we get a new email in our inbox, or our wife frowns at us, or a thought of worry or anxiety flashes through our mind. Anything can be a "something happens." And when something happens we "drift" out of presence. Instead of being in the flow or in the zone, in peak performance, we are now just off. Something has changed. Our energy starts to go flat, our body and breath constrict and we start to become reactive and triggered. Our buttons are beginning to be pushed. This state we call a "drift."

DRIFTING

All leaders can resonate with the difference between being in presence and being in a drift. Drifting can look and feel many different ways.

See examples of drifting on next page.

EXAMPLES OF DRIFTING

DEVELOPED WITH HENDRICKS.COM

BLAMING
CONCEALING
WORRYING
COMPLAINING
GETTING TIRED
SPACING OUT
CORRECTING
IGNORING
EXPLAINING
INTERRUPTING
INTELLECTUALIZING
FACEBOOKING
RUSHING
COMPARING
TRYING HARD
INTERPRETING
WHINING
CARE TAKING

BEING SARCASTIC
GETTING CONFUSED
GETTING OVERWHELMED
GETTING SHY
ANTICIPATING
WAITING
REHEARSING
WATCHING TV
GETTING EMBARRASSED
DISMISSING
SEEKING APPROVAL
PROCRASTINATING
GETTING ENLIGHTENED
SHOPPING
ORGANIZING

SPACING OUT
CLEANING
SMILING
ASSUMING
BEING MISUNDERSTOOD
GETTING RIGHTEOUS
LOOKING INTERESTED
WITHHOLDING
SEXUAL ACTIVITY
DRINKING AND DRUGGING
EATING
EMAILING
COMPULSIVE WORKING
CHECKING MY PHONE

The issue for leaders is not "will we drift?" We will! The issue is how long do we stay in a drift before we shift. Everyone drifts, not everyone shifts. People who really get stuck in a drift find themselves in the drama triangle. Again, the issue is not, "Do leaders get into the drama triangle?" We do! The issue is how long do we stay in the drama triangle before we shift. Leaders are always drifting and shifting. Shifting is the master skill of all conscious leaders. This book is all about how to shift.

Once conscious leaders have accepted themselves for being in a drift or a defensive, reactive state, they ask themselves the second key question: "Am I willing to shift?" This is one of the most powerful questions leaders can ask themselves. The shift is from being closed to open, defensive to curious, and committed to being right to committed to learning.

SHIFTING

Shifting is a master skill of conscious leaders. We find that they practice it like professional golfers practice putting. In our experience, shift moves are a reliable way to move from a closed to open consciousness. Shift moves can be put into two categories. Shift moves that change our blood and body chemistry and shift moves that change our consciousness. When we are triggered or reactive our blood chemistry changes. The fight flight chemical cocktail courses through our veins and the body assumes reactive postures. Before we can shift our consciousness, the way we are seeing and being with our experience, we need to shift our blood and body chemistry. The first two shift moves reliably do that.

Conscious breathing: Whenever we're in a threatened and defended state, we hold our breath or breathe shallowly. A conscious breath shifts our breathing pattern and breaks the hold of our reactivity. Four conscious breaths with a four second inhale and a four second exhale deep into our belly literally shift our blood chemistry and breathing pattern.

Radically changing our posture: When we're defensive and more interested in being right than in learning, we each assume certain body postures. Most of us with a moment's thought can identify a defensive posture. Literally, defensive thoughts require certain body postures. So, by significantly shifting our posture we shift our defensiveness.

Once we have shifted our biology and neurology we are available to shifting our perspective. Trying to shift our perspective while still being amped on adrenaline and cortisol is impossible. This book is all about shift moves. Each chapter contains at least one. The shift move we want to introduce you to at this point is wonder.

WONDER

*Wonder is both a shift move and a state of consciousness. Effective leaders learn to get into a state of wonder on a consistent basis. What is wonder? To find out—and to see it in action—we need look no further than at a child. Before the age of six, children are natural wonderers. It's as though they move through the world saying, "Hmmm... I wonder what this is or I wonder how this works—or tastes or feels or smells—or I wonder what happens if I do this?" Wonder is open-ended curiosity. It is asking a question for which we don't know the answer, and we don't know—or care—if there is an answer. Wonder is as much about the question as it is about the answer.

In our experience, most leaders replace natural wonder with "figuring it out," a very different consciousness. Figuring it out presupposes that there is AN answer and the goal is to use the mind to find it. You can experience an example of "figuring it out" by solving a word puzzle.

*BASED ON THE WORK OF THE HENDRICKS INSTITUTE.

Unscramble the following letters to form a word:

N E I C E S N

To really get a sense of what "figuring it out" energy is like for most leaders, you would need to set a timer and give yourself a defined time to come up with the answer. In fact, you would need to give yourself a very small amount of time, far less than you think you'd need. You would also need to make this a win/lose game with significant stakes for winning and losing. Having done all this, you would have introduced anxiety and fear into the game and replicated the common business environment. Your brain chemistry would respond accordingly and adrenaline would surge through your system.

So, ticktock, ticktock, ticktock. What's the answer? Everybody else reading this chapter already has the answer—why don't you? (Comparing yourself to others is also an essential part of the fear-based environment.) This is not to say that figuring things out is unimportant. But it is not wonder, and it is not really as much about learning as it is about being right by finding the right answer. (By the way, the right answer to the word scramble is "incense.")

Wonder is a very different experience. It is not about figuring anything out. It begins with a willingness to explore and step into the unknown, which involves taking a risk and letting go of control—not an easy commitment. Once we're willing to be surprised by the unknown, the next step in accessing wonder is to ask a wonder question: an open-ended question that has no "right" answer.

Wonder is a very different experience. It is not about figuring anything out. It begins with a willingness to explore and step into the unknown, which involves taking a risk and letting go of control— not an easy commitment.

Wonder questions go beyond our current knowing, our past experience, and our current paradigms. Einstein was famous for asking wonder questions and then living in them. Leaders who are curious, above the line, and committed to learning ask lots of wonder questions. They make it a practice to generate them.

Here are a few examples of what might be wonder questions (remember that it's not so much the actual words of the question but the consciousness from which the question is asked):

- *I wonder what outrageous customer service would look like?*

- *I wonder what I can learn today that will benefit everyone?*

- *I wonder how we could get more done in less time?*

- *I wonder what choices I could make today that would allow me to experience greater and greater fun and creativity?*

- *I wonder what I could do today that would allow for a breakthrough in my life?*

- *I wonder what I can learn from the issue that keeps coming up with my partner that would expand my leadership?*

- *I wonder how abundance is showing up in my life today?*

Conscious leaders practice these and many other shift moves.

DEDICATION TO SELF-AWARENESS

Conscious leaders are passionately committed to knowing themselves. This is the basis of their willingness to "regard every interaction as an opportunity to learn" and their willingness to source a state of curiosity and wonder. An astute person once said that all information falls into three buckets:

1. What I know

2. What I know I don't know

3. What I don't know I don't know

Though conscious leaders have a good grasp on what they know and are interested in what they don't know, they are inexorably drawn to what they don't know they don't know. When it comes to self-awareness, they spend their time in the unknown by opening themselves up to feedback. When most people think of feedback, they think of written or verbal comments given in a performance-review type setting. For us, feedback is much more than that. It's information coming to us from a limitless set of sources. For example, our bodies are giving us feedback all the time in the form of sensations and feelings as well as perceptions and thoughts. People are also giving us feedback all the time, and the vast majority of it is never verbalized.

One of our favorite and most reliable forms of feedback is results. They give us immediate feedback about what we are committed to at an unconscious level. We said under Commitment 1 that radical responsibility is looking at your results to see what you're actually committed to. This source of feedback is a direct channel to powerful self-awareness.

COMMITMENT IN ACTION

Remember our friend Sarah at the beginning of this chapter? She was a poster child for a lack of self-awareness, wonder, and curiosity. In the midst of her defensiveness, she directed her anger at Diana telling her, "I don't believe you live this conscious leadership stuff, because your body shows that you lack discipline." Sarah didn't appear to be speaking from love but from fear and self-righteous anger and was probably trying to hurt Diana.

It would have been so easy for Diana to blow off her comment and let it go. But we've noticed that skilled conscious leaders commit to learning from all feedback, regardless of how it's given. Indeed, they learn that the feedback they most react to has the most learning potential. Diana is a master at this. For this reason, it didn't surprise the people in The Conscious Leadership Group when she posted on our web page several weeks after her interaction with Sarah:

When I was at the last Foundation retreat, I got feedback from one of the participants that my body looked like I did not have discipline around food. I got really curious about the feedback. First I giggled inside thinking that if she knew how much I want to eat versus what I allow myself to eat, she would be in awe of my discipline... food is ecstatic to me, and my lusty personality wants MORE! MORE! MORE!

Then I got curious about what gift she was giving me and I found that there was a whole new layer of discipline I could be experiencing around eating and caring for my form. So I have used this woman's voice as a wonderful challenge and have devoted myself to a whole different kind of discipline. It's not willful but instead devotional. The results are surprising in that there has been a significant difference in my sensitivity and my intuition is markedly more keen. And the shape of my body changing is wonderfully fun!

PRACTICING
THE COMMITMENT

1. Commit to learning over being right. Decide that even though you will get defensive at times, you will make the choice to shift to curiosity whenever you recognize you're defensive and below the line. Also decide that you will consider everything in life as a learning opportunity and value learning above all else. Share this commitment with key people in your life and request their support.

2. Ask yourself regularly, "Am I above or below the line?"

3. If you are below the line, can you accept yourself for being just where you are?

4. If you're below the line, ask yourself, "Am I willing to shift?"

5. If you are willing to shift, choose a shift move to open yourself to learning.

6. Ask wonder questions. Keep a list and share them with people close to you.

IN A NUTSHELL

Commitment 1 and Commitment 2 are really the foundation for being a "By Me" leader. Commitment 1 says I'm done blaming and complaining and I see myself as the source of my experience. Commitment 2 says I value learning over being right. I value growing over the survival of my identity. I choose curiosity and wonder. These two commitments open a world of possibilities.

CHAPTER SUMMARY
Learning Through Curiosity

▶ Self-awareness and learning agility are known to create sustained success in leaders—they form the foundation of conscious leadership.

▶ Conscious leaders are passionately committed to knowing themselves, which is the basis of their willingness to live in a state of curiosity.

▶ At any point, leaders are either above the line (open, curious, and committed to learning) or below the line (defensive, closed and committed to being right).

▶ Being "right" doesn't cause drama, but wanting, proving, and fighting to be "right" does.

▶ Even though conscious leaders get defensive like everyone else, they regularly interrupt this natural reactivity by pausing to breathe, accept, and shift.

▶ The issue is not whether we will drift but how long we stay in a drift before we shift.

▶ There are two kinds of shift moves: those that change our blood and body chemistry (such as conscious breathing and changing our posture) and those that change our consciousness (such as speaking unarguably and appreciation).

Feeling All Feelings

I commit to feeling my feelings all the way through to completion. They come, and I locate them in my body then move, breathe, and vocalize them so they release all the way through.

I commit to resisting, judging, and apologizing for my feelings. I repress, avoid, and withhold them.

The boardroom was filled with thirty senior leaders charged with directing their billion-dollar, 11,000-person organization. They had come together to discuss the findings of a prestigious consulting firm hired to identify several hundred million dollars worth of cost cutting over the next few years. This wasn't the first time these leaders had seen the recommendations, but it was the first time they were going to determine which ones to implement and when. We had been invited to help facilitate the conversation.

This successful organization, like many others, is directed by visionary, smart, driven, passionate, and analytic leaders. To their great credit, they are very data driven. At this particular meeting, spreadsheet after spreadsheet of data lay before them, along with a PowerPoint presentation packed with recommendations and scenarios. Yet after several hours of talking, they had made little progress, and the CEO asked us to step in and support the discussion.

As we've observed in many organizations, these leaders were talking primarily from their head. In fact, for a majority of leaders, the head is the go-to center for conversation. But that's only one part of an effective decision-making process. We believe that great leaders learn to access all three centers of intelligence: the head, the heart, and the gut. In our experience, most leaders rely on their head and neglect the heart. This approach can be catastrophic because the heart center is the center of emotional intelligence. As Dan Goleman and many others have demonstrated, when it comes to sustaining leadership success, emotional intelligence (EQ) is just as important as IQ, if not more so.

Everyone in the boardroom had sufficient IQ to secure a seat at the table and probably at any corporate table. They also had the skills and competencies necessary to do their job and do it well. What they lacked, and what many leaders lack, because until recently it had not been considered a priority, was superior emotional intelligence, the ability to lead from the heart center along with the head and gut.

This organization was about to do what many do: make rational, objective decisions (or at least what they believed were rational, objective decisions—more about this later).

They would have missed the importance of feelings in leadership. Then they would have announced these decisions to the company with a compelling "burning platform" motivation about why they needed to do the difficult work of reducing expenses.

They would have been consciously or unconsciously living the "To Me" component of Commitment 3:

I commit to resisting, judging, and apologizing for my feelings. I repress, avoid, and withhold them.

Again, in our experience, this is standard operating procedure in most organizations. Feelings are resisted and often repressed because they're viewed as a distraction to good decision-making and leadership.

Let's explore the more effective approach contained in this commitment.

I commit to feeling my feelings all the way through to completion. They come, and I locate them in my body then move, breathe and vocalize them so they release all the way through.

EMOTIONAL LITERACY

For the last twenty years, a growing body of research has argued convincingly that emotional intelligence is essential for great leadership. But before you can become emotionally intelligent, you must first be emotionally literate.

Achieving emotional literacy involves two steps: (1) developing a clear, accurate definition of emotion and (2) identifying the core emotions.

Let's begin with a definition. What is an emotion? Such a basic question seems more appropriate for kindergarten than an executive development program, but in our experience, most people struggle to define it.

Here is a definition we like: Emotion is "e-motion." Energy in motion. At its simplest level, emotion is energy moving in and on the body. Or said another way, feelings are physical sensations.

Stop and think about this.

Whenever you experience an emotion, you feel a sensation in your body (thoughts, pictures, and sounds are often present, but not always). Anger has a certain set of sensations, as does sadness and fear. Your feelings are these sensations—there is no difference.

From our perspective, understanding this most basic definition is critical. If an emotion is merely energy, or a sensation, moving in the body, then it is neither good

Feelings are resisted and often repressed because they're viewed as a distraction to good decision-making and leadership.

nor bad, right nor wrong—it just is. That means we are not our feelings any more than we are our hunger pangs or the discomfort associated with a sprained ankle. Feelings just occur.

The second step to emotional literacy is being able to identify the core emotions. All colors come from three primary colors: red, yellow, and blue. Every other color is a combination of these three. Similarly, we suggest that there are five primary emotions—anger, fear, sadness, joy, and sexual feelings—each with a unique energy pattern or set of sensations in and on the body.

For example, when we refer to the feeling of anger, we are including low-intensity anger like upset, tense, annoyed, dissatisfied, displeased, frustrated, irritated, bothered, and bored (yes, from our perspective, boredom is usually anger we aren't facing or expressing). We also include moderate-intensity anger like agitated, aggressive, belligerent, disgusted, indignant, irritated, resentful, and revolted; as well as high-intensity sensations like embittered, enraged, furious, hostile, infuriated, seething, and vengeful.

Fear, sadness, joy, and sexual feelings have comparable gradations. In our work with leaders, we find it helpful to label all sensations along the continuum from low to high intensity, with the simple core feeling they match, e.g. angry, sad, scared, joyful or sexual.

Many other words can describe the nuances of these five feelings and what occurs when they are combined. For example, hurt can be a combination of anger and sadness, guilt a combination of fear and sadness, and jealousy a combination of fear, anger, and sexual energy. From our perspective, it's useful to identify the core emotions underneath all emotional experience.

LOCATING FEELINGS

With this basic understanding in place, we can begin to develop emotional intelligence. To help leaders do that, we follow a practice of pausing in the conversation and asking them, "What are you feeling right now?" This powerful question invites people to look beyond thinking and see what is occurring in their heart and body. It sounds like a simple question, but it's more difficult than you think.

For example, when leaders are asked, "What are you feeling right now?" many respond with such statements as, "I'm feeling that if we make this decision, it will have devastating consequences," or "I feel like you're missing the point," or "I feel that your data isn't accurate." Notice that even though these sentences begin with "I feel," they are actually thoughts, judgments, beliefs, or opinions. They are not feelings.

The primary learning is this: When asked to check in with current feeling states the accurate answer is "I feel..." followed by one or more of the five core emotions. If the words "I feel" are followed by "that" or "like," you are expressing a thought, not describing a feeling.

Once leaders identify a feeling, we ask the next coaching question: "Where is that feeling in your body?" Again, this takes people out of their head and into their body. Learning to locate and describe the sensation is the beginning of moving from emotional literacy (the basics) to emotional maturity.

We learned from two of our mentors, Gay and Kathlyn Hendricks, that the core emotions/sensations tend to show up in certain regions of the body. For example, fear often manifests as a sensation in the belly (like butterflies in the stomach), whereas anger appears in the back, shoulders, neck, and jaw, as well as down the arms to the hands. We typically experience sadness as a sensation in the heart area, the front of the throat and face, and in the eyes. Joy is often experienced as a rising, effervescent sensation in the core of the body or up the spine, and sexual feelings are typically experienced as tingling sensations in the erogenous zones. For those more sensitive to sexual feelings, this tingling sensation can be spread throughout various parts of the body. Learning these emotional zones of the body can be a shortcut to emotional maturity. When you feel a sensation in one of these areas, check to see if the corresponding emotion is present. Let the body lead you to awareness.

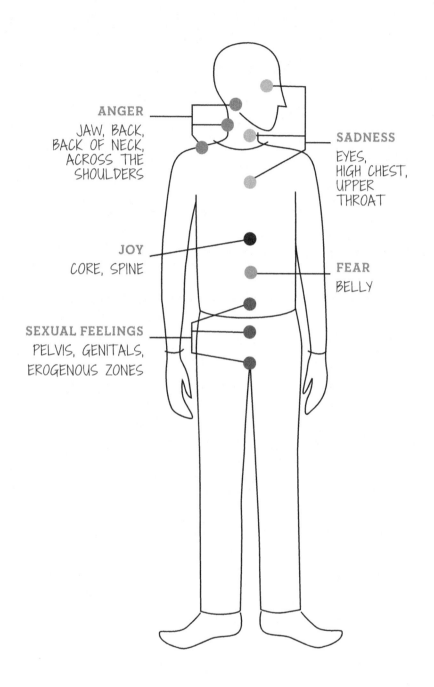

ANGER
JAW, BACK,
BACK OF NECK,
ACROSS THE
SHOULDERS

SADNESS
EYES,
HIGH CHEST,
UPPER
THROAT

JOY
CORE, SPINE

FEAR
BELLY

SEXUAL FEELINGS
PELVIS, GENITALS,
EROGENOUS ZONES

DEVELOPED WITH HENDRICKS.COM

REPRESSING AND RECYCLING EMOTION

This commitment is not just about locating and naming feelings. That is just the first step. The real mastery comes from being able to fully release those feelings.

Feelings are supposed to be released. In fact, they release themselves naturally and spontaneously if we don't prevent it. Human bodies naturally release. We take in a breath and let it go. We take in food and water and expel them. Unfortunately, we have been trained to keep emotions from doing the same.

Instead of releasing emotion, we hold on to it. One way we do this is by repressing it, denying to others and ourselves that we are having a feeling. Often in our coaching, we'll say to a leader, "You look and sound angry. Are you feeling angry?" The repressed response: "No, I'm not angry," said with a red face, bulging veins in the neck, a clenched jaw, and a raised voice.

Repression is a typical response to most emotion. If you look back at your childhood, you'll undoubtedly recall messages you received (often communicated nonverbally through behaviors) that emotions, especially some emotions, were not acceptable. Depending on your family, you might have been taught that feeling sad was okay but you could never feel anger. Or you could feel anger but sexual feelings were taboo. Very few of us were raised by caregivers who understood that feelings are just sensations that need to be experienced and released. Most of us discovered that when feelings were felt, something bad happened. For example, when Dad got mad, somebody got hurt. Therefore, we learned to suppress emotion, deny feelings, and block the free flow of emotional energy.

Here is one significant observation about repression. When we repress one emotion it can often influence the flow of other emotions. The five emotions flow through the body as water does through a hose. If you kink the hose, water stops flowing or slows to a trickle. Similarly, if you kink your emotional "hose" (repress emotion), all emotions are affected. Many people would like to block anger but still feel joy, or they'd like to limit sadness but still have sexual feelings. This is very difficult to do.

In addition to repression, we frequently prevent the natural release of emotions by recycling them, which occurs when we get stuck in a cognitive/emotive loop. Cognition is thinking and emoting is feeling. When our mind gets involved, we create an endless loop that causes emotions to recycle rather than release.

Often in their journey, leaders learn that repressing emotion causes all kinds of problems physically, psychologically, and relationally, so they shift from repression to expression. When done properly, expressing emotion is a key to releasing it. But expression can often be a part of recycling emotion.

For example, during a performance evaluation, your manager tells you that you must improve your presentation skills or risk being passed over for promotion or, even worse, possibly terminated. Upon hearing this, your stomach knots, heat rushes to your face, and your jaw clenches, indicating fear and anger. They are just naturally occurring sensations in the body, energy in motion. If you are adept at feeling your feelings, you can release them. If you are not skilled, you either repress the emotions, denying that you feel anything and running from them in a myriad of ways (numbing out, drinking, shopping, eating, working, watching TV), or recycle them by using your mind to keep them going, like stoking the fire by blowing on the embers. You do this by compulsively having thoughts like these:

- *My manager has no right to make such an evaluation. He's only heard me present twice.*
- *If I lose my job, I'm in big trouble.*
- *I knew I should have taken that speech class in college.*
- *This is all happening because that one client complained to my boss and I made a few mistakes in one presentation.*

Instead of focusing on the body and feeling the emotions, you intensify them by replaying all kinds of mental models. We call this drama-based or thought-generated emotion. When people get stuck in this drama, energy never gets released.

RELEASING EMOTION

Releasing emotion is radically different from repressing or recycling. Releasing involves the following steps:

LOCATE THE SENSATION IN YOUR BODY. Bring your attention to the sensation and describe its precise nature as accurately as possible. We like to tell people to imagine that their body is made up of billions of "bits." Ask yourself this useful question, "What are the bits doing?" Words like twisting, popping, tightening, spinning, and flowing are good descriptions. Be as specific and as granular as possible.

BREATHE. So simple, yet so profound. We know that when feelings occur, especially when they are intense, we alter our breathing pattern, which freezes the emotion in place and restricts its release. Once the sensation is located, take a few gentle full breaths, breathing as deeply into the belly as possible.

ALLOW, ACCEPT, OR APPRECIATE THE SENSATION. Begin by simply allowing. Ask yourself the question, "Can I allow these sensations to be here?" If you can, go beyond that by accepting or even appreciating the sensations, but just allowing them is sufficient. Remember that allowing emotion is the opposite of resisting or repressing it.

MATCH YOUR EXPERIENCE WITH YOUR EXPRESSION. Earlier we said that expression was key to releasing emotion, but not just any kind of expression. If you call a coworker and complain about your boss and your performance review and talk about how afraid you are that you're going to get fired, you are actually recycling the feelings and that won't help release them at all. You'll get stuck in thought-generated, drama-based emotion.

In contrast, the expression that we promote involves moving, breathing, and vocalizing to match the sensation occurring in or on your body. Matching is the key. This occurs by asking yourself, "If this sensation could make a sound, what would it be?" and "If this sensation could move, how would it do that?" The body releases naturally when you vocalize and let it move to match energy. By vocalization, we don't mean "talk about it," because that usually leads to recycling. Rather, we just mean make a sound.

We intuitively understand this because we see babies and animals do it all the time. Beings who aren't encumbered by the ability to think obsessively about feelings simply release them. Babies cry, dogs growl, and cats hiss. They naturally match experience with expression and release emotion. Babies and animals don't hold on to feelings. They let them go.

This matching of experience (what is the sensation) with expression (move and vocalize) is important for releasing feelings. Leaders learn to check their body, match their experience, check their body, and match their experience, going back and forth until the energy is released.

In her book *My Stroke of Insight*, Harvard-trained and published neuroanatomist, Jill Bolte-Taylor says that emotions last at most ninety seconds. We agree. Most emotions—sensations occurring in and on the body— move through the body in a minute and a half or less (usually far less) if we match our expression with our experience. If you repress or recycle emotion, it can harden into a mood: Anger becomes bitterness. Fear becomes anxiety. Sadness becomes apathy. And these moods can last for years.

It is also our experience that emotions come through the body in waves, similar to waves on the shore. An emotion rises, crests, and releases (if we release it), followed by a period of calm, still spaciousness, which is often followed by another wave. In times of intense emotion, these waves can be quite large (tsunami-like) and close together. At other times, they are merely ripples on a glass-like surface of water. Learning to release feelings is the key to experiencing the calm spaciousness that is always in and around the next wave. Once leaders understand emotion in this way, they are free to actually enjoy the waves (the sensations) and experience the calm. For some who have been practicing for a long time, the experience of any and all emotions/sensations can be delightful, but in our experience, this level of emotional maturity is radical and rare.

Feeling a feeling all the way through (the main objective of Commitment 3) means letting that feeling have its full life cycle (less than ninety seconds) by breathing, moving and vocalizing, resting in calmness, and riding the next wave through to completion.

THE WISDOM OF FEELINGS

All three centers of intelligence—head, heart, and gut—give tremendous knowing to a leader. The wisdom of the heart center, of emotional intelligence, is essential to great leadership, but typically goes untapped. So what exactly is emotional wisdom?

From our perspective, each of the five core emotions invites us to grow in awareness and knowing. Here are some of the learnings each emotion can give a leader:

ANGER: Anger tells a leader that something is not, or is no longer, of service. Or, that something is not aligned, and must be changed or destroyed so that something more beneficial can replace it. This emotion tells a leader that a boundary needs to be set or an existing one is being violated. Without access to anger, leaders are dangerous because they don't have a clear "NO." They don't have a "sword" for cutting and destroying when both are called for.

We recognize that some people will have a negative reaction to the phrase "cut and destroy." At the same time, we believe that great leaders know that eradication is occasionally necessary, as in eliminating old beliefs, old ways of relating, and old ways of seeing the world. Nature understands this and is not afraid to destroy something no longer sustainable. Destruction opens the possibility for new birth—when a wild fire burns a dead forest, the heat releases the seeds into the newly created fertile soil. That is the intelligence of anger.

We are not referring to an abuse of power that would be committed by insecure leaders attached to their ego. Rather, we encourage "cut and destroy" actions from a leader with an open heart, in service to the greatest good. When conscious leaders move from anger to eliminate what is no longer of service, they very often don't look angry on the outside. There is no outburst. There is only

Feeling a feeling all the way through (the main objective of Commitment 3) means letting that feeling have its full life cycle (less than ninety seconds) by breathing, moving and vocalizing, resting in calmness, and riding the next wave through to completion.

the clarity that comes after they have identified anger and let it move through the body.

This conscious anger is distinct from unconscious anger, or anger below the line. Anger below the line looks like blame, righteousness, and criticism. Conscious anger is devoid of these three qualities.

FEAR: Fear tells a leader that something important needs to be known. One form involves something that is not being faced. Fear is the body's way of saying, "Wake up!" Like the pedestrian who comes to a curb and feels a wave of fear run through his body as he sees an oncoming car run a red light. Leaders who lack access to this fear are dangerous because they don't adequately sense danger and are often living in denial of reality.

A second form tells a leader that something new wants to be learned. Fear invites your full attention and presence. For instance, a leader's first negotiation is not too different from a driver's first experience behind the wheel of an automobile. The fear says, "Get here and present. You don't fully know how to do this and it will require all of your awareness." Again, without this fear, leaders, like sixteen-year-olds (without this fear), are dangerous to themselves and others.

This conscious fear is different from unconscious or toxic fear, or fear below the line, which is almost always about a made-up future state. It is anxiety disconnected from the present moment. It is lying in a warm bed with a full stomach visualizing being homeless and hungry one day and then becoming paralyzed or activated by this imagined possibility.

SADNESS: Sadness tells a leader that something needs to be let go of, said goodbye to, moved on from. Sadness is the energy of loss. Something once meaningful is going away. It could be a person, a dream, a vision for the company, a belief, an opportunity. Leaders who can't feel sadness are dangerous because they hang on to old ideas, people, projects, and dreams long after they have served their purpose. Also, such leaders have a very difficult time connecting with people at a heart level, a critical missing piece of their leadership.

Sadness below the line is always connected to a belief in "poor me"—I'm suffering because of what is happening to me. This unconscious sadness can last for hours, days, or years. Instead of a ninety-second wave that moves through the body, it is more like a boulder buried at the bottom of the ocean.

JOY: Joy tells a leader that something needs to be celebrated, appreciated, or laughed at, or someone needs to be patted on the back. Countless leaders fail to create a culture of celebration and appreciation because they're cut off from their joy. In our experience, people are as afraid of feeling their joy all the way through to completion as they are their fear, anger, sadness, and sexual feelings. They mistakenly believe that it is inefficient or boastful to feel this emotion. Leaders who can't experience joy are dangerous because they can't adequately celebrate and appreciate themselves and others, unconsciously committed to limiting things that would be celebratory.

Joy below the line looks like circumstantial happiness: I'm happy because the circumstances outside me are good. If the circumstances change, my happiness changes. On the other hand, authentic joy is based on a deep experience of internal well-being. We actually call it "uncaused joy" because it just is. Be aware that many people paste a smile on their face or fake a happy attitude when they're actually feeling fear, anger, or sadness. This is a denial move and has nothing to do with authentic joy.

SEXUAL FEELINGS: Sexual feelings are the energy of creativity and creation. They tell the leader that something new wants to be birthed, to be created, to come into the world. Think of a leader and a team as being pregnant with ideas and innovations. Because of the abuse of sexual feelings in the workplace, our society has tried to legislate them out of that environment. We understand the reason behind this but we believe that in doing so, we have limited creative potential.

For the purpose of this discussion, we'd like to differentiate between sexual lust, which leads to a desire to have sexual relations with another, and sexual creativity, which leads to the birth of new ideas and innovative breakthroughs. We have actually known many people who have had sex without having any sexual feelings. In fact, they are having sex while feeling angry, scared, or sad or while repressing feelings so they feel nothing at all. Leaders and teams open to creative sexual energy often experience a flow of life force when a great new idea is being created. This flow (sexual energy) can show up as a tingling sensation in the erogenous zones.

Not long ago, we coached a leader who directed one of the largest creative agencies in the world before he was thirty-five years old. When he heard us talk about sexual feelings and the ability to separate creative sexual flow from typical sexual behavior, he had an aha moment. He recalled that his agency was filled with sexual energy and that people often confused the powerful creative collaboration of sexual feeling with choosing to have sex with each other. This failure to distinguish one from the other led to constant drama in his life and in the organization.

Leaders without access to their creative sexual feelings are dangerous because they demand creativity and innovation while limiting both because of their lack of sexual flow. This is a potential minefield, and an entire book (or two) can be written on the subject. Superior leaders know how to have sexual feelings in a way that is respectful to themselves and to everyone else, and they use this sexual energy to create and give life to their organization.

The practice of conscious leadership allows a leader to experience emotion fully, release it completely, and learn from it quickly. This triple benefit is transformational for great leaders and their organizations.

COMMITMENT IN ACTION

Let's go back to the board room where this chapter started. When the CEO of the organization asked us to step in, we told the leaders that thus far they'd been talking only from their head. We asked them if they were willing to involve the heart center as well to access all the wisdom that emotional intelligence could give them. They said yes.

Next, we asked, "What are you feeling right now? Let's all check in and report our current feeling state." We've worked with this organization for several years, so this was a familiar question—at many other organizations, it would have elicited a collective sigh, rolled eyes, and thoughts like, "Who cares what we feel? Feelings are irrelevant. Let's just make a rationale, objective decision. Why get all touchy-feely? That's a complete waste of time."

All thirty leaders checked in with at least one core emotion (anger, fear, sadness, joy, or sexual feeling). Most were feeling a combination of fear, sadness, and anger. We asked them to locate the feelings in their body, and then turn to the person next to them and describe what the bits were doing. At this point, the energy in the room changed dramatically as it often does when authentic feelings are named and located. It's as though the room collectively exhaled and relaxed.

We then asked them if they would be willing to release the feeling by matching expression and experience. The CEO led the way. He let out a big growl and pounded the table with his fist. Next, he took a deep breath, checked to see if the anger was released, did it again, and then smiled. He did all this without saying any words. There was no blame, no explanation of "why" he was angry, just release. By the way, this CEO is a hard-edged, competitive ex-marine who is increasingly accessing his heart center in his leadership, resulting in a powerful transformation of the organization's culture and a growing bottom line. Others followed suit, and in a matter of minutes, the energy/sensations were released (at least this wave of emotion).

The leaders were then asked to break into groups of three and tune into the wisdom of the emotion they were experiencing. If they were feeling anger, they were asked to wonder about what was no longer of service and needed to be destroyed. If they were feeling fear, they were asked to wonder about what they were supposed to "wake up" to, pay attention to, and learn from. If they were feeling sadness, they were asked to get curious about what they needed to let go of (beliefs, ideas, people, dreams, hopes, visions).

As you might imagine, these "wonder questions" provided the leaders with wisdom that differed significantly from what they obtained from analyzing spreadsheets and PowerPoint presentations. Both are necessary and neither is sufficient on its own.

A second exercise invited the leaders to get in touch with the feelings occurring in the organization as people anticipated cost cutting. They were asked to open their hearts and allow empathy for people's feelings to be part of their decision-making process and communication. As they did this, whole new perspectives on what to do and how to do it emerged in the room.

Again, these leaders have practiced Commitment 3 for several years and have directly experienced the benefit of accessing the wisdom of the heart center by releasing feelings and learning from them.

PRACTICING THE COMMITMENT

To practice this commitment we recommend the following:

1. Stop periodically throughout your day and simply ask yourself the question, "What am I feeling right now?" The answer to the question must be one or more of the five core feelings: sad, scared, angry, joyful or sexual. Do not analyze the feeling and search for "why" you are feeling the feeling. Simply label it and then go back to doing what you were doing.

2. When a feeling arises pause and...

   - *Locate the sensation in your body. What are the "bits" doing?*

   - *Breathe and allow the bits to simply do what they do.*

   - *Move and/or make a sound to match what the bits are doing.*

DEVELOPED WITH HENDRICKS.COM

IN A NUTSHELL

Feelings are one of the universe's greatest gifts to human beings. They add richness and color to life. When emotions are understood (they are simply sensations occurring in and on the body), enjoyed and released (locate, describe, breathe, move, and vocalize), and wondered about with curiosity (what is this here to teach me?), they are a leader's essential ally.

▶ Great leaders learn to access all three centers of intelligence: the head, the heart, and the gut.

▶ Resisting and repressing feelings is standard operating procedure in most organizations. Feelings are viewed as negative and a distraction to good decision-making and leadership.

▶ Conscious leaders know that feelings are natural and expressing them is healthy. They know that emotion is energy in motion; feelings are simply physical sensations.

▶ The five primary emotions are anger, fear, sadness, joy, and sexual feelings. Knowing how to express them all of the way through to completion helps us develop emotional intelligence.

▶ Each primary emotion has a unique energy pattern and set of sensations in and on the body.

▶ Every feeling we experience invites us in a specific way to grow in awareness and knowing.

▶ Repressing, denying, or recycling emotions creates physical, psychological, and relationship problems.

▶ To release emotion, first locate the sensation in the body ("What are the bits doing?"), allow or accept the sensation ("Can I allow or even welcome these sensations?"), and then match your experience with your expression ("What sound or movement does this sensation want?").

▶ Conscious leaders learn to locate, name, and release their feelings. They know that feelings not only add richness and color to life but are also an essential ally to successful leadership.

COMMITMENT FOUR
Speaking Candidly

I commit to saying what is true for me.
I commit to being a person to whom others
can express themselves with candor.

---

*I commit to withholding my truth (facts, feelings, things
I imagine) and speaking in a way that allows me to
try to manipulate an outcome. I commit
to not listening to the other person.*

Tell the truth. Don't lie.

Seems so simple, so clear-cut, so obvious. But in our
experience (and probably yours), it's not. Research
shows that 97% of people admit to outright lying. In
our experience lying is a problem in many organizations
but not nearly as big of a problem as withholding.

WITHHOLDING

According to Jack Welch, leadership expert and former
CEO of GE, "the team that sees reality the best wins." In
our experience, seeing reality clearly requires all the team
members to be candid. But most firms and leaders practice
selective candor, or put another way, they withhold.

"Withholding" is refraining from revealing everything to all the relevant parties. By everything, we mean facts, thoughts (including beliefs, opinions, and judgments), feelings, and sensations.

People withhold facts:

- *I found an error in the spreadsheet that leads to faulty data. It's too late to do anything about it, and I'm afraid I'll get blamed if I tell my boss about it.*

- *One of our key clients has been meeting with our competitor and is seriously considering pulling their business from us. I think I can save them, so there's no need to alert people at my company at this point.*

- *I'm having sex with my secretary, but if I tell my wife, she'll leave me.*

People withhold thoughts (beliefs, opinions, and judgments):

- *In my opinion, it's a serious mistake to open a branch in the Northeast Region, but everyone else in the meeting seemed to think it was a good idea, so I simply gave the corporate "nod" and didn't say what I really thought.*

- *I have a judgment that our new sales associate is not being honest about his real level of experience, but I'm not his boss so I don't share it with the team.*

People withhold feelings, especially the Big Three: anger, fear, and sadness:

- *When I think about losing our Director of Operations, I feel afraid. She is a wealth of knowledge and experience, and I don't think she's easily replaceable, but the CEO wants us all to see the positives, so I don't reveal my authentic feeling.*

- *I feel angry when my boss shows up late again for our weekly team meeting but I don't reveal my feeling, because everyone says conflict is counterproductive and I'm scared of losing his approval.*

- *I feel sad when I hear that my colleague's son has cancer. In fact I can feel my eyes filling with tears but I blink them away and don't share my sadness, because sadness, especially crying, is a sign of weakness.*

People withhold sensations. Body sensations are often our first line of awareness in the world and a tremendous source of information, wisdom, knowing, and intuition:

- *Every time I've interviewed the candidate we're considering for head of distribution, I get a queasy feeling in my stomach that feels like nausea. I blow it off, thinking I've had too much coffee.*

- *When I hear our VP of Sales talk about next year's forecast, I feel a pounding in my chest and tension in my upper back and neck. I had the same sensations as a kid when my father used to promise to take us on vacations, even though I knew we didn't have the money to ever go.*

THE RAMIFICATIONS OF WITHHOLDING

In our experience, withholding creates serious problems for the leader as well as for teams and organizations.

For the individual who withholds, the major problem is a decrease in energy. Great leaders know that to bring their gifts fully to the world and to realize their vision, they need as much energy as possible. Energy, in this case, is the flow of life force, whether it be intellectual, emotional, physical, spiritual, relational, or economic. When we "withhold," this energy flow is dampened, or in some cases, blocked altogether.

From our perspective, withholding is not a moral issue (Thou shalt not lie and withhold because it is wrong!), but rather an energetic one. When we withhold, we cut ourselves off from the free flow of energy necessary for individual and collective creativity, innovation, and implementation.

REVEALING OR CONCEALING

At any moment, individuals and leaders are either revealing or concealing. They are either becoming more transparent or more opaque. In our experience, leaders who reveal (facts, thoughts, feelings, and sensations) have a free flow of abundant energy for accomplishing their vision. Leaders who conceal and withhold interrupt this free flow of energy in themselves and in their organizations.

Blocked energy shows up in many ways. One common manifestation of it in a couple, for example, is boredom or relational lethargy. Whenever one of us encounters this boredom in a relationship, we are fairly confident that they are withholding from each other. They are not fully expressing facts (I opened another charge account even though we agreed I wouldn't), thoughts (I think I'm getting old and becoming unattractive), feelings (I feel sad when I think about you leaving for a month for business), or sensations (When you touch me like that, I feel cold shivers down my back). Candor is one of the great antidotes to boredom. If couples learn to reveal rather than to conceal, boredom is rarely an issue in the relationship.

This also happens in the work setting. Boredom and lethargy are often symptoms of blocked energy resulting from withholding. One mark of a healthy culture is employee engagement, and in our experience, engagement and candor are directly correlated. When we block candor by withholding, engagement wanes as well.

So the first problem of withholding is energy depletion. The second problem is relational disconnection.

Another of our favorite models is:

REVEAL OR CONCEAL
DEVELOPED BY HENDRICKS.COM

Withhold ➡ Withdraw ➡ Project

vs.

Reveal ➡ Connect ➡ Own

In our experience, this model points to a principle of the relational world. In relationships we develop judgments, beliefs and perspectives about other people. People do things that we label good or bad. We like what they do or we don't. These labels or judgments are the normal work of the brain in relationships and life. For example, we judge colleagues as smart, capable, hard working, analytical, team-oriented, etc. We also judge them as weak, selfish, political, dull, manipulative, disrespectful, underperforming, etc. Both lists go on. In unconscious, below the line relationships, we develop these judgments, believe they are RIGHT and withhold them from the person we've judged. We withhold them for many reasons including:

- *We don't want to hurt their feelings.*
- *We don't want conflict.*
- *It wouldn't do any good to tell them anyway (because they'll never change).*
- *Nobody else in this culture talks about these things directly with other people so I shouldn't either.*

According to this relational principle, whenever we withhold, we withdraw. Initially, withdrawing is often subtle. We slightly pull back from the other. We no longer fully engage with them. Often we say to ourselves that this person cannot be fully trusted, justifying our disengagement. This withdrawal leads to the final step in relational disconnection: we project.

Projection, in this scenario, is seeing the other person through my judgments about them and believing them to be right. For example, I judge that my boss is disrespectful toward others and me. I withhold this judgment and withdraw a bit in the relationship. I don't trust him. From this place of withdrawal I see him through the lens of my judgment, which means that I see him as disrespectful. Once I see him as disrespectful, I look for evidence to confirm that I'm RIGHT about my judgment. And guess what? When I look for evidence to prove that he is disrespectful, I find it. What I seek, I find. Furthermore, I dismiss any evidence that would disprove my judgment that he is disrespectful. I unconsciously block it, discount it as an exception, or don't see it at all. As a result, I have more judgments about him being disrespectful and the pattern continues. I see another example that he is disrespectful. I withhold it. I withdraw further and I project my judgment onto him finding more and more evidence that I'm right. This is the vicious cycle of relational disconnection that is prevalent in many organizations.

Leaders who lead from above the line take another approach. They reveal their thoughts, opinions, judgments and feelings. These leaders realize that the mind generates all kinds of judgments about people, circumstances, situations and conditions. Again, this is just what a mind does. The conscious leader doesn't see his judgments as RIGHT. Rather, he simply sees that judgments are arising. He also notices that the judgments that arise are more about him than they are about the other person. Our judgments about the world tell us a great deal about ourselves and very little about the world. They reveal something about our reactions, beliefs, listening filters, unconscious habits or expectations.

In powerful committed relationships, where both parties share a commitment to candor and to deep listening, we encourage a practice of revealing judgments. The key is that we reveal our judgments so that we can make ourselves known. We don't reveal our judgments to be RIGHT or to change the other person. In other words, when I reveal my thoughts and feelings I'm telling you about me, not about you.

In the situation above, where an employee has the judgment that his boss treated him disrespectfully, he approaches his boss and says something like, "We have a commitment to practice candor with one another so I'd like to honor my commitment and reveal myself to you. I notice that I had the judgment that you treated me disrespectfully in yesterday's meeting when you interrupted me. My desire is simply to let you know the judgment arose. I don't need to be RIGHT about it and I know this is really about me. I wanted to reveal myself so that you can know me and so that we have the possibility of a connected relationship. I don't want to withdraw."

In our view, connected relationship is the second step in a conscious candid relationship. In relationships we control how much we reveal to the other person about ourselves and we control our level of acceptance when others reveal themselves to us. These are two powerful aspects of any relationship which are totally under our control. When we say to another, "I want to create the potential for connection with you, so I choose to reveal," we're doing all that is under our control to have a conscious relationship.

Finally, the third step in conscious leadership and conscious relationships is to own. In unconscious relationships we project: we put our internal experience on others and believe it is true about them. Ownership is the exact opposite. When we own our projections we see that our judgment about our boss that he was disrespectful is an insight we can own about ourselves. To own our projections we notice that a judgment has arisen about being disrespectful. Once we notice this we ask the following kinds of wonder questions from curiosity:

- *How am I being disrespectful in my life?*
- *How am I being disrespectful toward my boss?*
- *How am I being disrespectful toward myself?*
- *How is it as true or truer that my boss is being respectful of me?*
- *How am I requiring people, including my boss, to be disrespectful toward me?*
- *How do I create this and how do I keep it going?*
- *How am I not seeing the value of interrupting? I've made interrupting a bad thing and am I open to seeing how interrupting could be a good thing?*
- *Am I willing to see how interrupting could actually be a sign of respect instead of a sign of disrespect?*

Remember that wonder questions from curiosity require us to be genuinely open to insights that arise from this place of radical responsibility. For more ideas on how to shift away from projecting, read about Commitment 10, devoted to the exploration of how the opposite of my beliefs may also be true. From this place of owning our projections we become high-speed learners who grow and transform rapidly. We also become truly available to great partnerships both at work and in our personal relationships.

Before we leave this model we notice that every time we teach this paradigm a question arises. You are probably asking this question as well, "What if I act this way and my boss doesn't (or my husband doesn't or my children don't)? Aren't I setting myself up for trouble?"

To this question we have many responses but two are foundational. Initially, we suggest that you practice this kind of candor—reveal, connect, own—only when you have a shared commitment to candor. Commitment is a cornerstone of all relationships and in conscious relationships we get clear and explicit about our shared commitments. In the workplace this looks like having a conscious discussion with your team about what commitments you want to agree to at work. If you agree to practice the commitment of candor, then you have a laboratory where you can experiment and grow. If everyone doesn't have a commitment to candor, we recommend that you get clear with your work partners about which conscious commitments you share. In life, we also recommend practicing with people with whom you share a commitment to conscious living, and in this case, candor. The reason for this is that we want you to succeed. In our experience, your odds for succeeding in implementing and benefiting from this practice go up dramatically when you practice with people who are as committed as you to living consciously. At first, if you practice with people who aren't committed you run the risk of getting hurt, being rejected and misunderstood. We don't think this is useful to your learning process.

Our second response to the question is this: once you have been practicing in co-committed relationships and have developed some mastery of this skill, you can experiment with relating this way to people who don't know anything about candor. In our experience, when you do this you will learn many wonderful lessons. Two keys to this experiment. First, pick people with whom you would like to be closer. You are risking for the sake of closeness and connection. Second, don't practice candor in order to change the other person. If you're trying to change the other person by using any of the skills taught in this book, you're still below the line and will create drama. Remember, candor is about you revealing to learn about yourself and to build the potential for relational connectedness. Most people aren't interested in you trying to change them with all your fancy new consciousness techniques.

So withholding leads to low energy in the leader and relational disconnection in the team. The third challenge that results from withholding goes back to what Jack Welch said, "The team that sees reality the best wins." Notice that he refers to a team, not an individual. Most individuals distort reality based on their history, culture, and personality. Very few individuals see reality perfectly. That is why teams are so important. If we all speak candidly and don't withhold facts, thoughts,

*If we all speak candidly and don't withhold facts,
thoughts, feelings, or sensations, it greatly increases
the probability that collectively we can see reality
more accurately.*

feelings, or sensations, it greatly increases the probability
that collectively we can see reality more accurately.
Revealing by itself, though, won't make that happen—
it must be combined with deep listening, presencing,
and curiosity. But without revealing, there is little
to no chance a team can see reality clearly.

So if we want to have abundant energy, (individually
and collectively), relational and team connectedness,
and see reality clearly, we need to practice candor,
thus the fourth commitment:

*I commit to saying what is true for me. I commit to being a
person to whom others can express themselves with candor.*

THREE CIRCLES OF CANDOR

What exactly is candor?

Most people believe that candor is "telling the truth." Certainly telling the truth is an essential part of candor, but in our experience, there's more to it than that.

THE THREE CIRCLES OF CANDOR

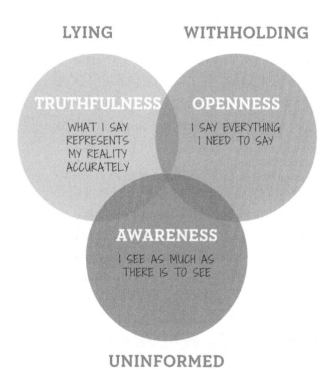

LYING   WITHHOLDING

TRUTHFULNESS   **OPENNESS**

WHAT I SAY   I SAY EVERYTHING
REPRESENTS   I NEED TO SAY
MY REALITY
ACCURATELY

AWARENESS

I SEE AS MUCH AS
THERE IS TO SEE

UNINFORMED

When we think about candor, we think about three overlapping circles. The first circle is the circle of truth. When we speak from the circle of truth, we tell the truth as we see it. If we're not speaking from this circle, we're lying or distorting the truth. Let's say that your boss asks you what time you got to work. Your watch said it was 9:15, and if you say anything other than 9:15, you're not in the circle of truth.

The second circle is the circle of openness. Being open and being truthful can be two different things. Most people believe that we're candid if we tell the truth and don't lie, but down deep, they know that candor also involves openness. Openness addresses the question of how much we reveal, whereas truthfulness addresses the accuracy of our reveal. If a colleague asks you who you had lunch with and you report that you had lunch with a friend from high school (and you did), that would be truthful. If, however, you fail to mention that the same friend is now a recruiter and she was talking to you about a job opening at another company, then you aren't being open.

The third circle is the circle of awareness. The first circle answers the question, "How accurate was my reveal?" The second circle answers the question, "How complete was my reveal?" The third circle answers the question, "How self-aware am I?" It's possible to be truthful and open but not fully aware. Again, if your boss asks you what time you arrived at work and you say 9:15 because that's what your watch says, you are being truthful and open. You are reporting reality as you see it and not concealing relevant information. If, though, your watch battery died and your watch stopped at 9:15 and you really arrive at 9:40 but didn't know it, you are being truthful and open but not aware.

A blind spot we encounter in leaders also involves projection. We talked about projection as part of the withhold, withdraw and project pattern, but here we see it again as a tool for self-awareness. Projection is a psychological defense mechanism, and like most defense mechanisms, it was designed to save our lives—or at least the life of the ego. Think of the mind as a movie projector and the world as a movie screen. Rather than face our own reality, we frequently project it onto the world, attributing our feelings, behaviors, and motivations to other people. This leads to major distortions. To grow in awareness, the third circle of candor, we must learn to recognize our projections.

For example, we recently coached a leader who was certain that a few of his peers were out to get him. He worked in a political environment filled with intrigue. As we coached him, something became clear: He was definitely out to get his peers. He spent significant amounts of time working to position himself in the best light and to cast others unfavorably. More importantly he was initially blind to this behavior. Rather than face it in himself, he projected it onto them and believed it to be true about them.

Let us be clear. Our client's peers might very well have been out to get him, but his inability to see it and own it in himself exacerbated the degree to which he saw it in others. Learning to "eat" your projections is a master skill of conscious leaders. We accomplish this by listing our beliefs and complaints about others and then asking ourselves, "How is this true about me? How am I not facing this in myself?" In the Twelve Step movement they have a wonderful motto, "You spot it, you got it." This simple phrase explains projection.

From our perspective, all three circles are necessary for the practice of candor. As we grow in candor mastery, we become more honest, more open, and more aware.

SPEAKING UNARGUABLY

Another key part of our understanding of candor is "saying what is true for me." A different way of saying this is that candor calls for revealing what is "unarguable," a powerful and useful distinction. Most "To Me" leaders, who lead from victim, villain, or hero, spend a majority of their time in drama about what is highly arguable. In fact, all drama in the triangle revolves around what is arguable and a commitment to being "right" about it. Great leaders learn to reveal what is true for them by revealing what is unarguable.

Based on the work of The Hendricks Institute, three types of reveals are unarguable: a thought, a feeling, or a sensation. By unarguable, we simply mean that people can't argue with it.

For example, if you say, "We have to get a new head of our department of surgery," that statement is arguable. Many could and would argue its truthfulness. Most suboptimal, drama-based conversations involve people arguing in an attempt to be right.

On the other hand, if you say, "I'm having the thought that we ought to find a new head of our department of surgery," that statement is not arguable. You are merely reporting the fact that you had a thought. That the thought occurred is unarguable. That the thought is true or right is highly arguable. Great leaders and teams become experts at revealing their unarguable experience ("I'm having a thought...") without forming any attachment to being right about it. They share it and are curious about it, but they don't need to defend it from an ego standpoint. When this candor is met with curiosity and deep listening "Tell me more about that thought. I'm curious to know what you think," amazing breakthroughs of insight and innovation often occur.

Here are three forms of unarguable communication:

1. I'm having the thought that...

2. I feel... [sad, scared, angry, joyful, or sexual].

3. I'm having a body sensation of... [pinching in my shoulder blades, swirling in my belly, throbbing in my temples].

Learning to differentiate between unarguable and arguable statements is a master skill of leadership and candor. Often simply saying something that is unarguable will end drama on the spot.

To speak with candor is to reveal what is unarguable with truthfulness, openness, and awareness.

One final point about candor. At any particular time, leaders are operating from either fear or love. This is simple yet profoundly true. Underneath all withholds is fear. We choose to withhold because we're afraid of losing approval, control, or security.

Conversely, candor comes from love. The Bible says, "Speak the truth in love." It couldn't be said better. Real candor is expressing the unarguable truth from love. When you develop a mastery of candor, you speak the unarguable truth to all relevant parties with thoughtfulness and kindness. Speaking from love is not a license to withhold or sugarcoat our unarguable truth, because we don't want to "hurt someone's feelings" (which is the most common reason people give for not wanting to be candid). Rather, speaking from love asks this question: "How do I say all my truth in the most loving way possible?"

Finally, when someone masters the practice of candor, the people they speak with often respond with curiosity and openness. In fact, one of the litmus tests of authentic candor is how others receive it. If people get defensive and argue with you when you're being candid, it's a good time to pause and make sure you're really saying what is unarguable and saying it in the most loving way possible. Sometimes the answer is yes and the other person is scared and therefore defensive, but it's a great practice to follow. This is combining candor with taking 100% responsibility.

> *Great leaders learn to reveal what is true for them by revealing what is unarguable.*

CONSCIOUS LISTENING

The commitment to candor includes two parts. The second is, "I commit to being a person to whom others can express themselves with candor." This part is equally important as being a person who speaks with candor. If you want to be someone who encourages candor in those around you, we suggest you practice the art of conscious listening. Conscious listening is one of the most important skills for effective leadership and, in our experience, most leaders still need a lot of practice in this area.

We learned from the Hendricks Institute that a filter is an internal lens that influences what we hear and how we respond. It translates a statement and gives it additional meaning, usually changing the way that the person responds. For example, we see many leaders listening to fix. This means a statement like, "I'm having trouble communicating with my director of sales," gets reinterpreted with a filter to fix it. In the "fixer's" head, it might sound like the person said, "How can you fix this communication problem I'm having with my director of sales?" The other person—of course—responds with solutions. Often the true intent of the statement, and certainly the speaker's emotions and desires are missed.

LISTENING FILTERS

Other listening filters we often see include listening to:

DIAGNOSE: "The problem with your director of sales is..."

CORRECT: "This isn't really a communication issue, this is an attitude problem."

AVOID CONFLICT: "I'm sure that they don't mean to be upsetting you; I'm confident you can work it out."

DEFEND: "Are you suggesting that I should have done something different with your director of sales!?"

PERSONALIZE OR HEAR HOW WHAT THE OTHER IS SAYING RELATES TO YOU: "I'm having a hard time with one of my top sales people. I wonder if it's something about those kinds of people?"

As long as these kinds of filters are being used, you are not understanding the true expression of the other person, so you will likely not be perceived by others as someone who listens to candor.

It takes courage to let go of listening filters and be fully present to what others are saying because you then must allow your own thoughts, emotional states and sensations. You have to be able to notice what is occurring in you, simply allow it to be there, and then shift your attention easefully back to the other. In a conversation, this occurs over and over.

> *One of the greatest gifts we give one another is to listen deeply to what the other person most wants.*

Most of us were taught that listening is simply about hearing the words or content that the other person is expressing. While this is one important aspect, we find that if you want to support candor, you also listen to what the person is feeling as they speak. The emotional intelligence required for listening depends on the practice of feeling your feelings (Commitment 3). The final aspect of listening is finding the core desire behind the content. What does the speaker most long for, want, or need?

We teach our clients to listen to the three centers of intelligence in another person. First you want to listen to the head center. What are the words, thoughts and beliefs you hear the other saying? If you really want someone to feel heard, do your best to repeat back exactly what you heard them say and be sure to get confirmation that you accurately heard them without leaving anything out or adding your own content.

Secondly, you listen to their heart center. What emotions are being expressed either directly or indirectly as they speak? Look for cues from their tone of voice, facial expressions or breath patterns. Do your best to reflect back to them how you imagine they are feeling. For this practice, it is important to be willing to get it wrong. Emotions often come in layers and reveal themselves after a few tries. Often, simply putting your attention on their emotions will help them contact their most authentic feelings.

Finally, listen to their gut or instinctive center. It is our experience that people often repeat stories because their base desire is not being acknowledged, either to themselves or others. One of the great gifts we can give one another is the reflection of awareness of what the other most wants. Often this is a revelation for both people. We've found that once core needs are acknowledged, conversations easefully shift to above the line resolution.

If you think you listen consciously, we encourage you to get feedback from others about how comfortable they feel revealing themselves to you. Most of us have blind spots about the listening filters we use that inhibit others' authenticity and unintentionally create topics or areas about which people withhold. This feedback allows you to continue fostering a community of complete candor.

COMMITMENT IN ACTION

If you want to see a team committed to candor, visit Research Affiliates in Newport Beach, California. CIO Jason Hsu, a brilliant and successful researcher, has spent most of his life avoiding conflict, being nice, and withholding. He leads a team of other gifted researchers, and in recent months, they have all made a commitment to candor. In fact, Jason requested that his team members and the other managers at Research Affiliates give him real-time, candid feedback. He asked for this feedback in writing or in person, whichever they preferred, and told them that they didn't need to be "right"—they could simply share their thoughts, opinions, beliefs, and judgments with him.

At first, his colleagues were cautious. After all, Jason is the company's second largest shareholder and the boss of many in the firm. But as Jason demonstrated sincerity, openness, and curiosity in response to candid feedback provided both in public and in private, people became more and more candid. They've told him they think he travels too much, has personal favorites on his team, and demeans non-investment professionals, to illustrate a few of the candid pieces of feedback. He has also received candid appreciation (often people withhold this).

As a result, Jason's self-awareness has grown tremendously, as has the trust between him and his team. Also, team members have been far more candid with one another in investment discussions, leading to better, faster, more innovative breakthroughs in research and product development.

Like most of us, Research Affiliates is toddling in its experience of candor, but make no mistake about it: Jason and his colleagues are benefitting from the flow of energy that comes from practicing candor.

PRACTICING
THE COMMITMENT

A key to the masterful practice of candor is learning
to speak unarguably. Here's how: practice completing these
sentences throughout your day. Begin by simply saying them
to yourself and then you can practice saying them out loud to
others who are committed to practicing candor:

I'm having the thought that...

- *We could do a better job with our recruiting effort.*
- *You're not giving us your full attention.*
- *The game should have turned out differently.*
- *My daughter doesn't respect me.*

I feel... [sad, angry, scared, joyful, or sexual]

- *The key to this practice is to answer only with feeling words. We recommend using the big five listed above.*

I notice... [report a sensory experience in or on the body]

- *Tingling in my right arm.*
- *Pressure in my shoulder.*
- *A pinching sensation in the front of my forehead.*
- *Heat rising up the center of my chest.*

DEVELOPED WITH HENDRICKS.COM

IN A NUTSHELL

For us candor is a simple yet profound commitment to reveal and not conceal. Our commitment is to reveal our stories, holding them lightly and expressing them lovingly. At any moment we are either choosing to reveal or to conceal. When we choose revealing we're choosing trust. When we choose concealing we're choosing control. Trust is rooted in love and control is rooted in fear. We believe love-based organizations win over fear-based organizations.

CHAPTER SUMMARY
Speaking Candidly

▶ Leaders and teams have found that seeing reality clearly is essential to being successful.

▶ In order to see reality clearly, leaders and organizations need everyone to be truthful and not lie about, or withhold, information. They need candor.

▶ Candor is the revealing of all thoughts, feelings, and sensations in an honest, open, and aware way.

▶ Speaking candidly increases the probability that leaders and teams can collectively see reality more clearly.

▶ Withholding is refraining from revealing everything to all relevant parties.

▶ Withholding also decreases energy in leaders, which often shows up as boredom or lethargy in them and relational disconnection in the team.

▶ Rather than withholding, conscious leaders practice revealing. They reveal not because they are right, but because they wish to be known. Through this transparency, they create connection and open learning.

► Conscious listening is one of the most important skills for effective leadership: by identifying our listening "filters," we can let go of them and become fully present to the expression of the other person.

► Conscious listening takes courage: we must listen for the content (head center), the emotions (heart center), and base desire (gut center) being expressed by the other person.

► It is best to start with candor in relationships only when you have a shared commitment to it, along with the necessary skills, including being able to speak unarguably.

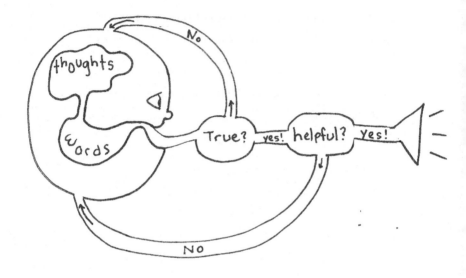

Eliminating Gossip

I commit to ending gossip, talking directly
to people with whom I have a concern, and
encouraging others to talk directly to people
with whom they have an issue or concern.

---

*I commit to saying things about people that I would
not or will not say to them. I commit to talking about
people in ways I wouldn't if they were in the room.
I commit to listening to others when they gossip.*

Gossip has long been a part of our culture. It even has its
own industry that generates millions of dollars each year
by producing tabloid magazines, television shows, and
tell-all books. Gossiping is also an accepted practice in
many organizations.

Because gossip is subject to several interpretations, we
want to clearly define what we mean by it. For our
purposes, gossip is either...

- *any statement about another made by someone with
  negative intent, or*

- *any statement about another that the speaker would
  be unwilling to share in exactly the same way if that
  person were in the same room.*

In our view, people who gossip like this are attempting to validate the righteousness of their thinking. They lack curiosity as they speak and are firmly planted within the drama triangle as a victim, villain, or hero.

Equally responsible are those who listen to gossip. Agreeing to listen to gossip is the same as speaking it. We liken gossip to a ping-pong game: the speaker and the listener each hold a paddle. If a listener says he doesn't want to listen and symbolically puts down his paddle, the game is over. So the listener is just as responsible as the speaker.

We regularly see articles that espouse gossip in the workplace, claiming that it is beneficial for two reasons: (1) It gets unspoken information out into the open, which apprises leaders; and (2) it allows people to release pent-up negative energy so it doesn't explode. The belief is that it's better to have a gossip mill than drive these statements underground, and it's better to vent than repress.

We understand this position; however, it's based on three assumptions:

1. People won't tell the truth to one another.
2. People don't know how to release negative energy in a healthy way.
3. It takes too long to thoughtfully process the information and feelings.

These are suboptimal ways to deal with these issues. Our work with clients has shown that candor and authentic feeling expression are more effective in the long term health of the organization. Issues get resolved faster, relationships are more trustworthy, and solutions are permanent and created with less energy.

A PR firm we once worked with had a toxic gossip problem that was sabotaging the creative potential of the entire organization. One member of the top executive team disagreed with the way the CEO was running the business and spent hours gossiping to whoever would lend an ear to her judgments. Many of her teammates were becoming enthralled with the drama, which—as everyone knows—can be very addicting because of its high entertainment value. They were spending more time talking about how right they were than developing dynamic PR campaigns. Others were feeling very "at the effect of" the gossip and losing morale.

Gossiping is a key indicator of an unhealthy organizational culture and one of the fastest ways to derail creativity. It takes a lot of mental and emotional energy to engage in stories about others, energy that could be used more productively for creating win/win solutions and advancing an organization.

The CEO recognized that the issue was getting out of hand when clients began dropping away. These clients were sensing a lack of cohesiveness in the creative team and didn't want to suffer the potential consequences of the drama. We were called in to help them address the problem.

!?

WHY DO PEOPLE GOSSIP?

Like all our behaviors, gossiping gives us certain paybacks that motivate us to continue. Most of them are unconscious. Here are a few of the top "benefits" we've identified:

MAKE OTHERS WRONG. Many of us relate to others from a one-up or one-down position: I see you as either less than me or more than me. Gossip is a favorite way to engage in one-upmanship, relieving us from feeling inferior.

GAIN VALIDATION. The ego lives in a world where we are either right or wrong. Since we don't want to be wrong, gossip allows us the opportunity to validate our righteous perspective.

CONTROL OTHERS. By gossiping, we feed our judgments to others, manipulating the information flow and attempting to control their beliefs and behaviors.

GET ATTENTION. Absent something meaningful to share with others, people may choose to reveal a critical or private story about someone else to draw attention to themselves.

DIVERT ATTENTION. When someone feels vulnerable, gossip is a great way to shift the attention to someone else. For instance, if kids are getting in trouble, they will distract by pointing the finger at another: "Hey, did you see what Carson did?!" Or people might gossip about the lives of movie stars instead of facing what is not working in their own life.

AVOID CONFLICT. We see this as a popular reason for gossiping in organizations. When people are concerned that their opinions or preferences are going to upset someone, they often vent them to people not directly related to the issue, such as spouses, friends, or other team members.

People may also choose to listen to gossip to avoid the discomfort of establishing a boundary. Outside our community of conscious leaders, we seldom hear someone say, "I prefer that you share this judgment directly with the person you are speaking about and not with me." Or "I am willing to listen to your issue with John to offer you feedback, as long as you are willing to clear the issue directly with him."

AVOID FEELING AND/OR EXPRESSING AUTHENTIC EMOTIONS. In many organizational cultures, fear, sadness, and anger are not honored as valuable emotions to have when "doing business."

For example, Judith, the head of marketing, does not agree with the decision of her teammate, the director of engineering. In fact, she is fuming! She believes that he is jeopardizing the business of one of their top clients. But rather than expressing her concerns and authentic anger to him directly, she stays mute during the meeting and waits until she is in the privacy of her own team to spout off about how wrong he is.

CREATE (PSEUDO) ALLIANCES. Some researchers propose that gossip has a healthy bonding aspect, suggesting that friendships can be born between those who share their grievances with one another. On the contrary, we believe that alliances rooted in shared victimhood compromise the well-being of the individuals and the effectiveness of the team.

WHEN IT'S NOT GOSSIP

Some people interpret this commitment as saying, "I'm not allowed to talk with anyone about anybody." And with that interpretation, we're often asked, "What about coaching or strategizing, or when I'm concerned?"

It is not gossip if your comments are serving the people you're discussing. If you can have the conversation without any sense of making them wrong, it is more likely a constructive exchange. Verify this by testing to see if you have a high level of curiosity. Then run the statements through this two-part test:

1. Is there any negative intent? If so, stop. You're gossiping.

2. Would you be willing to speak directly and in exactly the same way to the person? If not, stop. You're gossiping.

Talking about someone else can be beneficial when you want the best for that person and it is rooted in love—for example, talking with your spouse about the best interests of your child or talking to a manager about the future prospects and developmental needs of an employee.

HOW TO CLEAN UP GOSSIP

Both the gossiper and listener must take steps to eliminate gossip:

REVEAL TO THOSE TO WHOM YOU HAVE BEEN GOSSIPING: Margaret, I want to acknowledge that I have been speaking critically about Sarah to you without sharing my thoughts directly with her. I see that my behavior is not serving me, you, or Sarah, and I am committed to no longer gossiping about her to you or anyone else. I also plan to take responsibility for this issue by revealing to Sarah that I have been gossiping about her and clearing my issues with her directly.

REVEAL TO THE PERSON ABOUT WHOM YOU HAVE BEEN GOSSIPING: Sarah, I want to acknowledge to you that I have been speaking critically about you behind your back, and I feel regretful about my choice to do so. My relationship with you is important, so I'd like to clear an issue I have had with you directly. Is now a good time?

REVEAL TO THE GOSSIPER TO WHOM YOU HAVE BEEN LISTENING: Brian, I want to acknowledge that I have been participating in gossiping about Jim by listening to you criticize him. I no longer want to listen to any of your thoughts about Jim that you are unwilling to share directly with him. I am also unwilling to participate in any conversation about him where the intention is to make Jim wrong in any way. If it would be supportive, I'd be happy to facilitate a clearing conversation between the two of you.

We use a clearing model with our clients as a first step in helping them speak directly to one another instead of gossiping. In the model, we've illustrated each step with how it might sound in a conversation between Brian and Jim.

SEPARATING FACT FROM STORY

FACT

That which is unarguable, e.g. people don't argue with it

WHAT A VIDEO CAMERA WOULD HAVE RECORDED

FACTUAL AND OBJECTIVE DESCRIPTION

BLACK AND WHITE

REALITY

STORY

That which is arguable, e.g. people argue with it

OPINIONS

BELIEFS

JUDGMENTS

INTERPRETATIONS

MOTIVATIONS

ASSUMPTIONS

In order to use a clearing model effectively, it's important to understand the difference between fact and story. You'll be using both of these concepts if you clear with another person.

Facts are objective data. Facts are what a video camera would record. If you look at a video of a meeting, it contains sounds and images. It records words being spoken, including tone, inflection and volume. It also records gestures, body language and facial expressions. All of these are facts. Facts are unarguable. They are just what happened without any meaning.

Stories are interpretations of the facts. Stories include all judgments, opinions and beliefs that we derive from the facts. The way the mind works is that it takes in facts/data and then it makes up stories about the facts. All stories are made up. They are not TRUE. They are simply the way we see the world. Conscious leaders make a clear and constant distinction between facts and the stories they make up about the facts. They make sure that all facts are out on the table and then they encourage the expression of stories. They create a culture where stories (opinions, judgments, beliefs) are all welcome. They also create a culture where it is understood that stories are made up by the story maker and that they are not true. Although stories aren't true, they are incredibly valuable. They just are not facts.

Often we'll be in a meeting and we'll hear people say, "The fact is…"

- *They dropped the ball.*
- *We screwed up.*
- *This idea is dead in the water.*
- *He spoke disrespectfully to me.*
- *Legal and compliance are too oppositional.*
- *She's the best sales manager we've ever had.*

Actually, none of these are facts. They are all stories. The issue is compounded because many organizations—and rightly so—want to be data-driven. A high premium is placed on facts and data but these "facts" are really made up stories.

Conscious leaders know that facts are not the cause of upset or drama. Facts don't cause stress. Drama and stress are caused by stories, and stories are made up. We are the story maker. This is not to say that all stories cause drama and stress. Some stories make us happy. In the clearing model, it is not the fact that causes relational dislocation with a business colleague, rather it is the story you create about the facts.

This is liberating both personally and collectively. Once you understand that you and others make up stories all the time, and then believe that your stories are actually facts, you are free to shift. The shift move is to choose to hold your story lightly. Holding your story lightly means acknowledging that your story is YOUR story. It is not fact; it is not true; and you don't need to be right. It is simply the way you see the world. This facilitates sharing your stories and welcoming others to reveal their stories about the world.

THE CLEARING MODEL

In the clearing model it is critical to differentiate facts from stories. Both are part of the clearing model but they are separate. As with any expression of candor, The Clearing Model is effective when used from a mindset of care and curiosity. The structure of the model guides the conversation to address gossip and create a new understanding.

For this model to be effective all parties involved must have an experience of being "clear." So, at the end, when you are asked, "Are you clear?" what we mean is, "Have you said everything you have to say and felt everything you have to feel about this issue? Are you fully expressed?" To say that you are "clear" doesn't mean that the issue is resolved. It means that you no longer have any unexpressed thoughts, feelings, judgments and desires. It also means that you are willing to take your 100% responsibility for how you have helped create the situation and kept it going. Once you are clear you are able to have a conversation to resolve whatever is left that still needs to be resolved."

HOW TO SEPARATE FACT FROM STORY

FACT	STORY
Quarterly sales are down 4%	The sales team isn't doing their job
My manager spoke to me with a red face and increased volume	My manager is mad at me and disappointed in the job I did
A colleague came to a meeting at 11:15 that was scheduled to start at 11:00	My colleague doesn't respect my time or care about the subject of the meeting
I got a 22% bonus	The company thinks I'm doing a great job and they are pleased with my efforts
I wasn't invited to a corporate cocktail party	My team leader doesn't like me and doesn't value my input
I was fired	This is a BAD development

THE CLEARING MODEL

AFFIRM A MEANINGFUL RELATIONSHIP: "Jim, I want to clear this issue with you because I value our business relationship."

ESTABLISH A TIME TO TALK: "Is now a good time to talk?" "If not now, when?"

"THE SPECIFIC FACTS ARE..." (Recordable facts; not judgments) "The facts are that for four of the last five meetings, you showed up after the start time."

"I MAKE UP A STORY THAT..." (I imagine...; My story is...; My judgment is...) "I make up a story that this meeting isn't important to you. You aren't prioritizing this project, and because you're overcommitted, it will fall through the cracks."

"I FEEL..." (Angry, Sad, Scared, Sexual, Joyful...) "I feel scared and angry."

"MY PART IN THIS IS..." (My role in creating or sustaining the issue) "My part in this is that I didn't speak directly to you the first time it happened. I also didn't create a clear agreement with you at the onset about the timing or priority of these meetings. My own fear about completing this project is making everything feel significant."

"AND I SPECIFICALLY WANT..." "I want to make clear time agreements with you and renegotiate them beforehand, if necessary. I would really like you to check in with yourself to see whether you are aligned with this project and to tell me if you aren't."

PERSON B (JIM) LISTENS TO UNDERSTAND

"WHAT I HEAR YOU SAYING..." (Reflect or paraphrase without interpretation.)

Reflect back each section of person A's (Brian's) clearing. Match that person's words as closely as possible. The value of mirroring exactly is that the person experiences being listened to. The second is that when a person (in this case Brian) hears their own words repeated back they may realize that what they said is not what they mean.

So Jim would say to Brian, "What I hear you saying is that when I was late to four meetings, you made that mean that I wasn't committed to the project and that with my priorities as they are now, this project might fall through the cracks. You feel scared and angry. You see that we lacked a clear time agreement and that you feel heightened awareness around this because of your own fear. You want us to have clear time agreements for the future and for me to check about my own commitment to the project as a priority."

AFTER REFLECTING, ASK, "IS THAT ACCURATE?"
(If not, reflect again.)
"Brian, did I get that right?"

"IS THERE MORE?" (Ask in a kind, genuine, curious voice.) Ask the question "Is there more?" to verify that you have addressed the complete issue.
"Brian, is there any more about this?"

"ARE YOU CLEAR ABOUT THIS?" (If yes, move on.
If not, go back to "Is there more?") If person B (Jim) has an issue, A and B switch roles (Jim clears with Brian).

THE COMMITMENT IN ACTION

Let's circle back to the PR firm we mentioned at the beginning of this chapter. We spent a day with the entire firm discussing their challenges with gossip. Several team members revealed that it was difficult for them to speak honestly to the CEO about complaints they had with him. The CEO was surprised to hear this news and committed to staying open to any feedback the group had to offer him.

Using the clearing model above, we supported the company in expressing unsaid thoughts and unfelt emotions. The energy in the room noticeably improved as the gossip was revealed publicly to the group. At the end of the day, we asked all the members of the organization if they were willing to enter a company-wide agreement to end gossip. Everyone agreed, and the CEO made it clear that he would not collaborate with anyone who chose to break the agreement.

Several months later and after a warning, two team members were asked to leave the firm because of their incessant gossiping. We went back after they had been let go and detected a perceptible difference of well-being in the culture. We also learned that the CEO was receiving more direct feedback from others in the firm and that profits were up.

PRACTICING THE COMMITMENT

Begin to eliminate gossip from your interactions by committing to yourself and to key people in your life that you will no longer gossip. This is a simple and profound commitment.

Then, identify any areas in your life where you have gossiped and use the clearing model described here to clean them up. For some, this practice alone has revolutionized their relationships, resulting in great leaps in their leadership both at work and at home.

IN A NUTSHELL

Conscious leaders recognize the cost of gossip to their organizations and shift so that expression is done instead with candor and authentic feelings. They free up creative energy and collaboration, which can't exist while gossip is present.

CHAPTER SUMMARY
Eliminating Gossip

▶ Even though gossip has long been a part of office culture, it is a key indicator of an unhealthy organization and one of the fastest ways to derail motivation and creativity.

▶ Gossip is a statement about another made by someone with negative intent or a statement the speaker would be unwilling to share in exactly the same way if that person were in the room.

▶ Gossip is an attempt to validate the righteousness of a person's thinking and is below the line; it is not a comment designed to serve the person being discussed.

▶ People gossip to gain validation, control others and outcomes, avoid conflict, get attention, feel included, and make themselves right by making others wrong. In short, people usually gossip out of fear.

- If you gossip, clean it up by revealing your participation in the gossip to everyone involved.

- Use the issue-clearing model as a tool to separate fact from story and to learn to speak directly to one another.

- When leaders and teams learn to speak candidly with each other, they benefit from the direct feedback about issues within the organization that otherwise could derail creative energy and productive collaboration.

Practicing Integrity

I commit to the masterful practice of integrity, including acknowledging all authentic feelings, expressing the unarguable truth, keeping my agreements, and taking 100% responsibility.

I commit to living in incompletion by withholding my truth, denying my feelings, not keeping my agreements, and not taking 100% responsibility.

Several years ago, we worked with an investment firm that wanted to create a high-performing culture. We did an initial off-site with all fifty employees. Everyone seemed quite engaged as we talked about the qualities and practices of conscious leaders and high-performing teams. They asked us to return to support them in the work of transforming their organization. During that second visit, we met with top leaders and small groups to begin the practices of conscious leadership. Very quickly, we sensed that something was off.

We were coaching people in the practice of candor, teaching them about the power of revealing versus concealing, of holding their "story" lightly and speaking unarguably. It was obvious to us that some employees were resisting this practice. We often experience such resistance at first, but this time, it was palpably different.

During a follow-up phone call, several of the leaders let us in on the "secret" beneath the collective resistance to practicing candor. The proverbial "elephant in the room" was the CEO's affair with his secretary. Everybody in the firm knew about it. He was keeping the affair from his wife and trying to keep a secret from his partners at work, all the while publicly espousing the value of candor and telling his colleagues that the firm's success depended on all of them being candid.

This is an example of what we call an integrity breach, an infraction frequently committed by unconscious leaders. Most people would agree that the CEO was out of integrity. In our culture, having an extramarital affair is considered a major breach of integrity, as is the hypocrisy of telling others to be candid when you're not. Most people generally agree that these behaviors violate a moral or ethical code. The definition we often hear of integrity is "doing the right thing," and for the majority of us, the "right thing" is rooted in morality and ethics. So we are in integrity if we're moral and ethical and out of integrity when we aren't.

Much has been written and discussed about this understanding of integrity, and our purpose here is not to add to that conversation. Instead, we'd like to initiate a different conversation about integrity. We want to look at integrity not so much as doing the right thing or conforming to a moral or ethical code but rather as facilitating the flow of energy.

Let's begin with the basics. What exactly is integrity? Integrity means wholeness. The word "integrity" shares the same root as the word "integer," a whole number. When we say that integrity is wholeness, what do we mean? A combination of three elements: energy management, congruence, and alignment.

ENERGY MANAGEMENT

We have found that conscious leaders are masters at managing energy. When they allow energy to flow, they are alive, engaged, passionate, on purpose, creative, innovative, intuitive, clear, visionary, playful, relaxed, and refreshed. Energy flow is our natural state, but when it's blocked or interrupted, the life force so essential to great leadership is dampened, and effectiveness wanes immediately and drastically.

From this perspective, we want to define an integrity breach as anything that interrupts or blocks the flow of energy. Upon returning for our second engagement with the investment firm, we felt a collective block to the flow of energy in the company. It felt dead and lifeless. This is something people feel in their bodies and their hearts long before they understand it with their minds. Modern organizations spend millions of dollars and many hours on increasing employee engagement. We've discovered that engaging employees is all about allowing the flow of life force or energy in individuals and in an

organization. Integrity breaches are a major cause
of employee disengagement.

The flow of energy is like the flow of electricity, easily
illustrated with Christmas tree lights. Many of us have
had the experience of hanging a string of lights on a tree,
plugging them in with great expectation only to have
them remain unlit. At that point, the long and tedious
process of checking each bulb on the strand begins.
Once the offending bulb is located and tightened or
replaced, electricity is free to circulate through the
string, and the lights sparkle.

Energy works in a similar way. One integrity breach
interrupts the flow of life force, although in our case, the
light of the life force dims without completely going out.
This is not some new age voodoo about energy fields, but
rather a practical principle of leadership. The amount of
energy or life force leaders can support in their bodies
is directly related to their vitality, engagement, passion,
focus, creativity, innovation, intuition, clarity, and vision.

CONGRUENCE

Integrity is wholeness. One form of wholeness is the
uninterrupted flow of energy or life force. A second form
of wholeness is congruence, which relates to matching
what is on the inside to what is on the outside.

Congruence is a characteristic of powerful conscious
leaders. Yet many leaders believe that good leadership
calls for not matching experience to expression, or their
insides to their outsides. If they feel scared on the inside,

they do everything they can to avoid letting that fear show
on the outside. If they have a judgment or an opinion,
they're very careful not to express it. We understand this
belief—and the consciousness from which it originates—
but this is not congruence, wholeness, or integrity.

Leading from this old belief takes a tremendous amount
of energy. It takes effort to hold back feelings, thoughts,
wants, and desires. Our view is that leaders in today's
world need all their energy to lead, but many of them
expend their life force by blocking the natural flow from
the inside to the outside, from experience to expression.

Our bodies are meant to be open systems that "take in" and
"put out." Whether it is taking in food, water, or air, we do
best when we fully expel everything we ingest. Holding
your breath, for example, takes energy and is unnatural
and unhealthy. So, too, when leaders don't fully express
themselves to match their experience, it takes energy and
is unnatural and unhealthy. As you know from reading the
other commitments, we maintain that there are beautiful
and powerful ways to fully feel and express emotions,
thoughts, beliefs, and stories. Living those commitments
allows us to waste no energy blocking the natural flow of life.

ALIGNMENT

For us, then, integrity means the unbroken flow of energy, inside-outside congruence, and, finally, alignment. Alignment is about purpose and directionality. We are whole or in integrity, not just when energy is flowing and we are congruent, but also when we are "on purpose." Integrity is knowing what we're up to in the world and being in complete devotion to it. This purpose can change and often does. It doesn't have to be something great or grandiose, but it must be clear and compelling to leaders—clear enough for them to know at any moment whether they are on purpose and compelling enough that they passionately align their energy to fulfill it.

When we hold a Conscious Leadership Foundation retreat, everyone participates in an exercise on creating and declaring a life purpose. This powerful experience is only the beginning of the leader's growing clarity about what it is that he or she is up to in the world.

Integrity, then, is wholeness, and wholeness is...

1. The unbroken flow of energy and life force

2. Congruence between what is experienced and what is expressed

3. Alignment with life purpose

An integrity breach is anything that breaks our flow of energy, blocks the matching of our experience and expression, or moves us away from being on purpose.

A second form of wholeness is congruence, which relates to matching what is on the inside to what is on the outside.

FOUR PILLARS OF INTEGRITY

In practice, we have identified four pillars of integrity (we are indebted to Gay and Kathlyn Hendricks for this construct):

1. Take 100% responsibility
2. Speak authentically
3. Feel feelings through to completion
4. Impeccable Agreements

We have discovered that leaders who master these four pillars are probably living in integrity. Three of these pillars are discussed in other commitments. Commitment 1 is about taking 100% responsibility, Commitment 4 is about speaking authentically, and Commitment 3 is about feeling feelings through to completion.

So here, we'd like to explore the fourth pillar of integrity. From our experience, conscious leaders are impeccable in the way they handle their agreements. To understand what this looks like, let's begin with a definition.

An agreement is anything you have said you will do or anything you have said you won't do. It exists between two or more people. When you say to a colleague, "I'll get you the report by Tuesday at 5 p.m.," you have made an agreement. When you say to your spouse, "I'll pick up a gallon of milk on the way home from work" or "I won't have sexual relations with anyone else," you've made an agreement.

Agreements can be small ("I'll pick up a gallon of milk") or large ("I won't have sexual relations with anyone else"), but there is no difference from the standpoint of agreement impeccability. Energetically, failing to keep a small agreement breaks the flow of life force just as much as failing to keep a large agreement. This is not to say that all broken agreements have the same level of consequence in the world or produce the same amount of healthy shame internally, but all broken agreements break the flow of energy. Tom Peters, leadership and management expert, was correct when he said, "There is no such thing as a small breach of integrity."

When we say an agreement is between two or more people, the two people can be "me" and "myself." Many leaders are much better at being impeccable in their agreements with others than they are at keeping agreements with themselves. An agreement with yourself might look like this: "I agree to work out three times a week," or "I agree to meditate every day for twenty minutes," or "I agree to walk out of the office every day at five o'clock." Breaking agreements with yourself undermines integrity just as much as breaking an agreement with another. Both break the flow of energy.

We want to point out a distinction between an agreement and a commitment. A commitment involves a general direction of your life's orientation and is made between you and the universe. With commitments, you are either walking in the direction of your commitment or walking in another direction. For example, when we say, "I commit to the masterful practice of integrity..." we are saying that we are directing our life, moving toward integrity. At any moment, we can check to see if we are living this commitment or not. An agreement, on the other hand, is made between two people and includes who will do what by when.

IMPECCABLE AGREEMENTS

To be impeccable concerning agreements, this model asks us to master four practices:

1. Making clear agreements
2. Keeping agreements
3. Renegotiating agreements
4. Cleaning up broken agreements

MAKING CLEAR AGREEMENTS Making clear agreements first requires being very precise about who will do what by when. So many unconscious leaders are sloppy about this. For a blatant example, take the leader who says during a meeting, "Will someone look into that and get back to us?" There is no clarity around the who ("will someone") or the what ("look into that") or the when ("and get back to us").

Contrast that to the clarity of "Bill, will you analyze the impact of using USA Corp versus ABC Corp as our supplier, especially the impact on our inventory management, and get the report to us by noon on Wednesday?"

The second part to making a clear agreement is ensuring that everyone involved is fully committed to making it. Agreements are by definition bilateral, whereas assignments, demands, commands, and orders are unilateral. Conscious leaders know when to lead unilaterally and when to lead bilaterally. There is a time and place for both. If a leader is choosing to make an agreement, then he is choosing to invite buy-in—or what we call a whole body YES. This response is a total and unequivocal YES, with your mind, emotions, will, and body. For many leaders, teams, and organizations, it's a radical way to live. Instead of a whole body YES, many leaders practice the "corporate nod," nodding their head yes when they actually mean one or more of the following:

- *I don't really want to do that, but I can't say so in this meeting.*

- *I have no intention of doing that, but no one will ever follow up.*

- *Sure, I'll do it if I get to it, but I have a lot to do and this will fall low on my priority list.*

- *Let's just get this meeting over with so I can get back to work.*

Many people are not impeccable about agreements because they begin by making agreements they never plan to keep. In fact, we have noticed that this is the primary reason people get out of integrity with agreements in the workplace. We encourage leaders to teach their teams the practice of the whole body YES and to practice accepting and refusing agreements based on this awareness.

The third requirement for making clear agreements is keeping track of all the agreements you make. Gay Hendricks says that if your life is any more complicated than a Bedouin sheepherder's, you need to write down your agreements. David Allen's work *Getting Things Done: The Art of Stress-Free Productivity* is the best resource we know for learning how to keep track of your agreements in a complicated world.

KEEPING YOUR AGREEMENTS Simple enough. Do what you say you will when you say you will do it. Don't do what you say you won't do. Conscious leaders who are impeccable about their agreements keep about 90% of all the ones they make. You might ask, "Is 90% completion actually being impeccable?" Our answer is yes—if you follow practices 3 and 4.

RENEGOTIATING AGREEMENTS Renegotiating agreements means that as soon as you realize you're not going to keep an agreement, you communicate directly with the affected parties and renegotiate it. Renegotiation can include the following:

- *Deciding not to do the agreement at all*
- *Changing the scope of the "what" I'll be doing*
- *Changing the "by when" I'll be doing it*

Renegotiating sounds like this: "Bill, I told you I'd get the report done by Tuesday at 5 and I want to renegotiate with you. Can we agree that I'll have it done Thursday by noon?" It can also sound like, "Honey, I know I agreed to go to the Jones' with you for dinner on Friday night, but the more I tune in to myself, the more I recognize that I don't have a whole body YES to this. I'd like to renegotiate my agreement to go to the Jones' with you and them."

In our experience, people who are impeccable with their agreements renegotiate less than 10% of them. This renegotiation level is so low because they faithfully follow the first practice: Make clear agreements.

CLEANING UP BROKEN AGREEMENTS People who are impeccable with their agreements periodically fail to keep one and fail to renegotiate it as well. This becomes increasingly rare as leaders commit to agreement impeccability, but it does happen. To stay in impeccability, the leader must clean up the broken agreement, which can sound like this: "Joe, I told you I would talk to Kathy by Friday about the change in her role, and I want to let you know that I didn't keep my agreement with you. I realize breaking this agreement could damage trust with you, and I want to know if there is anything I can do to repair that."

Note that when cleaning up a broken agreement, you don't need to "explain" why you didn't keep the agreement. In the world of energetic integrity, explaining is a waste of time. The energetic loop is broken both internally and between two people when the agreement isn't kept. It doesn't matter why it wasn't kept. When cleaning up a broken agreement, first keep your statements short and simple: either "I didn't do it. I take 100% responsibility for not doing it" or "I did do it. I take 100% responsibility for doing it." Second, ask if there is anything you can do to clean up the broken agreement.

COMMITMENT IN ACTION

Sue Heilbronner is a conscious leader committed to living and leading from wholeness and integrity. Sue attended a Conscious Leadership Foundation retreat during which all the leaders were asked to get clear about their commitment to integrity. We asked them to really look and see if they were willing or unwilling to commit, either a whole body YES or a no. In our experience commitment always precedes knowing what this will look like or how we will act if we step into the commitment. People often want to know the "how" or the "what" before they commit. In our experience, the "how" and the "what" come after willingness. Wanting to know the how and what before we commit is like asking to see the movie before we buy the ticket. Commitment is buying the ticket. This comes first and then we get to see the movie.

Once Sue fully committed, she completed the Integrity Inventory, a simple and direct tool that allows us to see any integrity breeches we have in the four pillars of integrity.

▶ ▶

HERE ARE THE DETAILS:

EMOTIONAL INTELLIGENCE—UNFELTS

Have I felt all my feelings around...

- *My childhood*
- *My parents*
- *Any relationships that have ended*
- *My siblings*
- *My children*
- *My career*
- *My spouse*
- *My body*
- *My money*
- *My sexual orientation/desires*
- *How I use substances (drugs, food, alcohol)*
- *Death: mine and others*

CONSCIOUS COMMUNICATION—UNSAIDS

Is there anything I have been withholding from...

- *My spouse*
- *My children*
- *My extended family, parents, siblings.*
- *My friends: current and past*
- *My colleagues: current and past*
- *Myself*
- *Anyone else who comes to mind more than three times*

Is there anything I have been withholding about...

- *Emotions: anger, fear, sadness, joy, sexual feelings*
- *Agreements*
- *Judgments*
- *Desires, wants, requests*
- *Money*
- *Stealing*
- *Approval*
- *Comparison*
- *Lying*
- *Appreciation*
- *Sex*
- *Consumption: food, alcohol, drugs*

IMPECCABLE AGREEMENTS—UNKEPTS

Have I kept all my agreements with...

- *My spouse*
- *My children*
- *My extended family, parents, siblings,.*
- *My friends: current and past*
- *My colleagues, current and past*
- *Myself*
- *Anyone else who comes to mind more than three times*

THE DETAILS (CONT)

Have I kept all my agreements about...

- *Sex*
- *Money*
- *Time*
- *Things*

HEALTHY RESPONSIBILITY—UNOWNEDS

Am I blaming...

- *My spouse*
- *My children*
- *My extended family, parents, siblings.*
- *My friends: current and past*
- *My colleague: current and past*
- *Myself*
- *Anyone else who comes to mind more than three times*

Am I in victim or blame...

- *My past*
- *My present circumstances*
- *My lack*
- *My emotional states (anger, sadness, fear, joy, sexual feelings)*
- *My spiritual states*
- *My physical condition*

▶ ▶

Sue took an hour to complete the inventory. During the exercise, she saw clearly that she had broken an agreement—not a small agreement, but rather a significant one by most people's standards. Like most of us, when Sue faced this integrity lapse, she felt fear and deep regret. After feeling her feelings all the way through to completion, she faced the decision of whether she was willing to step into full integrity and clean up the broken agreement. Her choice was YES.

The next part of the process was extremely powerful for Sue and all of us. She excused herself from the meeting, went outside, and called the people with whom she had broken agreements. As is often the case, each conversation lasted less than ten minutes. First was the direct simple ownership of the broken agreement, "I did what I said I wouldn't do. I take full responsibility." Next was staying with the other people while they had their experience and expressed themselves fully.

When Sue returned to the meeting, her energy was obviously different. It was flowing, and it continued to flow throughout the rest of the retreat. She was fully alive and available to co-create with the other leaders at the retreat.

In preparation for writing this chapter, we asked Sue what her experience had been in the two months since she cleaned up the broken agreement. Here is what she said:

"Since my broken agreement crossed over from personal to professional, cleaning it up has produced what I feel are enormous gains on both fronts. For the people involved and me, it feels like a real call to integrity. Almost a sense

of 'Oh, this girl is serious about this integrity stuff... if she's willing in a ten-minute period to address something that seemed so big, then we know that we are all expected to deal with integrity breeches associated with the day-to-day work we do together.'"

"This action also opened me up to handling many other integrity breaches at work, including many examples of sharing my vulnerability and worry about decisions I make as a leader. I think that type of integrity would not have been open to me without the big cliff dive during the The Conscious Leadership Group retreat. Again, for me, revealing myself suddenly felt small, easy, low-hanging fruit. To my team, however, some of whom were not part of the original phone calls, the cleaning up of these integrity glitches does not feel small. My story is that they don't expect such candor and admissions of fallibility on the part of their leaders. I love how it opens them up to the same and how it shifts the balance on the team, giving more room for junior people to step in with their big ideas without fear of anything associated with the inherent "rightness" of being the boss."

"This revealing so completely was also incredibly powerful for the personal relationship that was affected. In that situation, the other person involved saw an opening to share his lapses in integrity. After his initial fury, he told me how much he appreciated finding all this out from me. He experienced the disclosure as a sign of respect for him and for the relationship we shared. Honestly, after years, I don't think our relationship has had a period of greater intimacy or candor."

In Sue's words, she expresses the flow of energy, life force, and positive outcomes that all people experience if they are fully committed to the masterful practice of integrity.

For those of you who are wondering about what happened to the CEO we talked about at the beginning of the chapter, he was unwilling to clear up his integrity breaches, so we stopped working with him and them as a client. This is an important point for us and for many conscious leaders. We realized that to continue to work with a client who was so far out of integrity would have interrupted the flow of our energy; we would have been out of integrity. It is very important for conscious leaders to pay attention to the level of integrity around them. This "field" of integrity effects everyone in it.

PRACTICING THE COMMITMENT

When it comes to practicing the commitment to integrity we know of no better practice than the one described above that Sue Heilbronner and many other leaders have participated in over the years. From our experience, this is not a practice that a leader does once and it is over. Rather it is a practice that we do over and over, like meditation or exercise. We believe conscious leaders are always cleaning up unfelts, unsaids, unkepts, and unowneds, returning to integrity.

IN A NUTSHELL

We believe that integrity is essential to conscious leadership. It is foundational. In fact, we contend that without it, there is no conscious leadership. Most of us would agree that integrity is important to leadership, but our view is that integrity goes far beyond simply "doing the right thing." It is living a life of wholeness. Conscious leaders who are in integrity are whole leaders. Whole leaders have a better chance to create teams and organizations that operate in integrity and to lead them to creativity, production and success.

CHAPTER SUMMARY
Practicing Integrity

► Integrity is the practice of keeping agreements, taking responsibility, revealing authentic feelings, and expressing unarguable truths. It is essential to thriving leaders and organizations.

► Integrity is not defined here as conforming to a moral or ethical code, but rather as facilitating wholeness and congruence.

► Integrity is an unbroken flow of energy and life force, congruence between what is experienced and expressed, and alignment with life purpose.

► Organizations have a natural flow of energy, but when it is interrupted by integrity breaches, leadership is dampened and employee engagement decreases.

- Conscious leaders are masters at managing energy, which leads to an organizational culture that is alive, engaged, passionate, on purpose, creative, innovative, intuitive, clear, visionary, playful, relaxed, and refreshed.

- There are four pillars of integrity: taking radical responsibility (Commitment 1), speaking candidly (Commitment 4), feeling all feelings (Commitment 3), and keeping agreements (Commitment 6).

- Conscious leaders are impeccable with their agreements. They make clear agreements, keep them, renegotiate them when needed, and clean them up when broken.

- Integrity is fundamental to conscious leadership and successful thriving organizations.

Gratefulasana

Generating Appreciation

I commit to living in appreciation,
fully opening to both receiving and
giving appreciation.

---

*I commit to feeling entitled to
"what's mine," resenting when it's not
acknowledged in the way I want.*

In 2007, the financial services industry was booming.
The stock market was climbing, wealth creation was easy,
and opportunities for financial advisors abounded.

At many of the firms we worked with, the management
began offering complimentary services to their employees
to keep them happy and motivated. They could drop off
their dry cleaning and have it delivered to their office.
A massage therapist came in for weekly appointments,
and the kitchen was always stocked with everyone's
favorite drinks.

At first it was exciting. Eating breakfast at work with an
endless supply of cereal choices was a novelty. But then it
became an entitlement. People expected exactly what they
wanted, when they wanted it. And if it wasn't there, the
complaining began:

"I work hard here. The company should provide a personal trainer for me at my gym. And I shouldn't have to buy my own membership. Don't they want me to stay in shape?"

"What do you mean I can't get in with the massage therapist? She should be here an extra day a week!"

"I can't believe the admin didn't buy Diet Dr. Pepper. She knows it's my favorite. Someone else must be drinking too much of it! There should always be plenty. I have a right to the drink I asked for being in the fridge when I open it!"

Times have changed since then, not only in these companies, but throughout much of the world economy, yet the culture of entitlement persists. When review season arrives, anything less than a 10% bonus is seen as a slap in the face: "That bonus is mine. When you hired me, you said I would earn more than I did at my old firm. (Never mind that I didn't perform this year, or that the stock market plunged.)"

In these conditions, comparison and jealousy start to enter the fray, along with a lot of mounting frustration. Many employees believe that they deserve a raise—that they earned it—for just showing up: "My compensation should increase every year because a year went by." Or

"I should make more than another person in my position because I've worked here longer."

While the official definition of entitlement once referred to legislated rights, it has come to mean a belief that a person deserves a particular reward or benefit. This notion typically starts with a preference—for soda, a bonus, or a service—which in itself is fine. The problem arises when we become attached to the outcome. Our preference turns into an expectation—not something we'd like to happen, but something that we believe should happen, and in a certain way. It is often a fast and slippery slope from wanting to deserving.

When we feel entitled, we are stuck in a "To Me" attitude, and the victim, villain, and hero roles come into play. As the victim, we are at the effect of someone else providing something we think we deserve. The villain in us would blame someone else for our dissatisfaction, believing that if they would just provide what they were supposed to, the problem would go away. In the hero mode, we would provide the entitlement to make people happy, at least temporarily, and avoid having to deal with any underlying difficult issues.

THE MEANING OF APPRECIATION

For our purposes, the definition of appreciation has two components.

SENSITIVE AWARENESS. The first step of appreciation is awareness: simply paying attention. That requires being present in the moment and bringing all of our attention to the person or situation. But sensitive awareness implies more than simply paying attention. It involves the capacity to make fine distinctions. For example, someone who appreciates art notices subtle differences and minute details, such as brush strokes, variation in color, and the effects of light and shadow. Similarly, a wine connoisseur, who appreciates wine, can detect fine flavor distinctions, from the wood of a barrel to the quality of the soil in which the grapes were grown. A layperson who doesn't fully appreciate art or wine overlooks these subtleties. "It's a pretty painting" or "What a tasty bottle of wine" are appreciations but they are a long distance from the statements made by someone with a fine-tuned awareness.

As you become a master of appreciation, you can make more and more refined distinctions, combining experience with the wonder of fresh eyes. The capacity for specificity becomes part of the delight. If you've been with a partner in relationship for a period of time, you can easily see the path toward and away from appreciation. With appreciation, you might notice a wrinkle that appears around the eyes when your partner truly laughs. Or the nuances of an idea that he or she has been exploring.

On the other hand, if you stop being sensitively aware, you miss noticing new things about your partner. Often we hear people say, "They're boring. He's been thinking about that same idea for years. She always laughs at the same jokes." To us this simply means they have stopped paying attention with fresh eyes.

AN INCREASE IN VALUE. When something appreciates, it grows in value. Someone who lives Commitment 7 has the intention of having their relations, circumstances, and experiences become more valuable. As you begin this journey of appreciation, this appears to require effort. As you develop mastery of this commitment, you will notice that this increase in value occurs easefully. It is from intention rather than effort that the appreciation occurs.

A CLOSER LOOK AT APPRECIATION

Like the definition, the commitment to live in appreciation has two branches.

FULLY RECEIVE APPRECIATION. In our work with leaders and teams, By Me leaders practice fully receiving appreciation. They know that their own ability to appreciate starts with their self appreciation and receptivity to others attention.

DEFLECTING APPRECIATION However, we've found that for many, it's more difficult to receive than to give appreciation. Usually unconsciously, they use internal and external strategies to refuse the appreciation.

A few favorite scenarios:

The Inner Critic Interception. Regardless of outward signs to the contrary, the recipient internally dismisses the appreciation. The inner critic says, "What he's saying isn't really true. He wouldn't be saying that if he really knew me. There are plenty of counter examples."

The Hand-Off. The recipient passes credit to someone else—"It wasn't really me. It was Paul over there"—or redirects the appreciation to someone else: "Oh, you think that's a gift of mine, but you should really be paying attention to Suzy; she has that much more than I do."

The Downgrade. The person responds by comparing herself unfavorably to an ideal that she didn't meet. "Well, this was okay, but it wasn't perfect. Next time, I'll do it better."

The Dismissal. The recipient diminishes the quality or action as unnoteworthy. "That was nothing. I hardly did a thing," or "That's not anything special. Everyone is like that."

The Reciprocation Race. The person reciprocates in kind: "Oh, you're the nicest person for saying that. And I appreciate you even more than you appreciate me."

We have discovered at the core of these strategies are several reoccurring fears about receiving appreciation:

- *If I receive appreciation I am going to have to give appreciation and I am not sure I have either the capacity or the desire to appreciate.*

- *They don't really mean it. They are just flattering me in order to get something from me.*

- *If I take in appreciation it requires me to be vulnerable and I don't want to expose any weakness.*

- *Receiving appreciation ups the bar of expectation and I am not sure I can live up to that every time.*

> *The first step of appreciation is awareness: simply paying attention.*

- *If I receive the appreciation I will get lazy and not improve myself.*
- *If I accept this appreciation it means I am not humble.*

Take a minute to find your own strategy for refuting appreciation and its root fear.

RECEIVING IS A GIFT. Think of appreciation as a valuable gift, something to be cherished. If a good friend came to your housewarming party with a gift, would you give it back to him and say you didn't want it? Or give it to someone else in front of him? Would you close the door and send him away? Most people wouldn't refuse a gift, yet they refuse appreciation, which is the emotional equivalent.

Refusing appreciation robs the other person of a chance to give you their gift. You cheat both of you out of an experience of growth and connection. And usually you deny a truth about yourself.

FULLY GIVE APPRECIATION. We can bestow the gift of appreciation to ourselves or to others. This is the practice of refining our attention and placing it on aspects of ourselves or others that we'd like to nurture.

To illustrate, try this exercise:

Look around the space you're presently occupying. Find every white item in a 360-degree view. Keep track. Make a mental note.

**STOP NOW AND ACTUALLY DO THIS
BEFORE READING FURTHER**

Now focus on just a sheet of paper (or your screen) and make a list of all the green items you saw. Then look around the room and see how much you missed.

What this exercise illustrates is that you notice what you are looking for. What you place your attention on grows. What would happen if you started observing people to catch them doing something good, rather than focusing on things they need to change or improve? What you seek, you will find.

This is not to say that giving constructive feedback is unimportant. It is (see Commitment 4 on candor for a discussion on effective feedback). Expressing appreciation is also important. Research continues to show that a ratio of approximately five appreciations for every one criticism comment is the optimal ratio for strong relationships.

THE FOUR ELEMENTS OF MASTERFUL APPRECIATION

A masterful appreciation must include these four elements:

1. **Sincerity.** Appreciation must be real and true. If it's not genuine it's not appreciation. Insincere comments often create more harm than good because people come to doubt the intention (Are you trying to manipulate me?). Masterful appreciation doesn't only involve your head (what you think), it also involves your heart (what you feel) and your body (what sensations you are experiencing).

2. **Unarguable truth.** Appreciation is most effective when it is unarguable (see Commitment 4). This prevents any judgments, comparisons, or conscious or unconscious challenges. In the context of appreciation, this is the difference between "That was a great report!" (arguable) and "I appreciate you for the detailed appendices in this report; I noticed how at ease I felt having all the information at my fingertips" (unarguable).

3. **Specificity.** Sometimes appreciation is expressed in vague terms, leaving the recipient guessing at its true meaning. "I like your shirt" can make the recipient wonder whether the statement referred to the color, fit, fabric, or some other attribute. Those practicing the art of appreciation use specificity and clarity.

4. **Succinct language.** A masterful appreciation can be completed in a single out breath, meaning everything you can say in one exhale. It's like

the best chocolate: a little goes a long way. And like chocolate, too much can spoil the experience. Additionally, once you go beyond one out breath, usually the appreciation becomes arguable.

COMMITMENT IN ACTION

Pat Christen and her team at HopeLab are dedicated to this commitment, and they have devised a multitude of ways to express appreciation to one another on a weekly if not daily basis. One of our favorite examples appeared at their year-end holiday party in 2012.

A couple of weeks before the event, the organization sent out to each staff member a list of their fellow team mates' names. Each member was asked to write three to five qualities that they most appreciated about each of their colleagues. These qualities were then gathered for each person and a list was made, which was then made into a word cloud (with the help of an internet app found at **www.wordle.net**).

At the holiday party, these word clouds were displayed around the room with the names of each person hidden behind a flap of paper. As the staff members wandered through this gallery, they were asked to guess which word cloud they thought was theirs. They also had a contest to see how many of the word clouds partygoers could correctly identify with the person they described.

One of the team members was new to the organization, so for her word cloud, the staff chose words to describe how they had gotten to know her during the interview process and included qualities described in letters of recommendation. She was shocked to see it and to find it so accurate.

We spent time with the group directly after this event, and so many of them shared their gratitude for the experience of being "seen" by their colleagues. Some were surprised by the qualities represented. One man with a twinkle in his eye said, "I had no idea how much my humor is appreciated here and how funny others think I am."

Chris Murchison, who often creates these kinds of experiences at HopeLab, has just released a collection of ideas on how to encourage appreciation and connection in the workplace. For more information on this project, visit **http://www.deckaholic.com/lib/check-in-deck** and check out their "Check-In Deck."

PRACTICING
THE COMMITMENT

If you'd like to enhance appreciation in your organization, try these four ideas:

1. Do the white/green (or other appropriate colors for your space) exercise (described earlier in this chapter) with your team to exemplify "What you place your attention on grows."

2. Place three dimes, heads up, where you can regularly see them. Every day commit to finding three people to appreciate. Whenever you deliver an appreciation (following the keys to mastery: sincere, unarguable, specific, succinct), flip the dime over.

3. Use this chart to come up with various ways to appreciate. Choose the method that feels most authentic for the person and situation you are appreciating.

SPOKEN	WRITTEN
PUBLIC	PRIVATE
EXPECTED	UNEXPECTED
PROFESSIONAL	PERSONAL

4. Do thirty days of corporate appreciation, which you can find on our websites.

IN A NUTSHELL

Appreciation allows us to recognize the unique gifts of both others and ourselves. It also supports the expansion of what is most valuable in individuals and organizations. Conscious leaders become masters at giving as well as receiving appreciation and are committed to showing gratitude even in the midst of great challenge and conflict.

CHAPTER SUMMARY
Generating Appreciation

▶ Committing to appreciation, along with avoiding entitlement, helps leaders and organizations grow value and connection in the workplace.

▶ Appreciation is comprised of two parts: sensitive awareness and an increase in value.

▶ Entitlement arises when rewards and benefits become an expectation instead of a preference.

▶ Living in appreciation has two branches: being open to fully receiving appreciation and being able to fully give appreciation.

▶ For most, it is more difficult, and people are more afraid, to receive appreciation than to give it. To avoid receiving appreciation, people strategically deflect it.

▶ Masterful appreciation is sincere, unarguable, specific, and succinct.

▶ Appreciation allows the unique gifts in the community to be recognized.

Excelling in your Zone of Genius

I commit to expressing my full
magnificence and to supporting and
inspiring others to fully express their
creativity and live in their zone of genius.

---

*I commit to holding myself back and not realizing
my full potential by living in areas of incompetence,
competence, and even excellence.*

It's a familiar story. Joe has a job that he does quite well. When he first started, he was really excited about it. He rose through the ranks to become COO. But for the last several years, work hasn't been all that he would like it to be. It's not horrible—it's just not fun or enlivening. Joe, like many leaders we work with, has lost his passion. Days blur into one another as he goes through the motions of a job he can do in his sleep.

He sometimes daydreams about the work he'd rather be doing: teaching history to high school kids, bringing to life the characters he's always admired, who have so much to teach us all. But there's no practicality in that. He couldn't support his family the same way. Besides, he's pretty good at what he does. To go back to school to get a teaching degree—that just seems crazy. Only twenty more years until retirement. It's not that long…

Joe, like many of the leaders we meet, is committed to holding himself back and not realizing his full potential.

UNDERSTANDING THE ZONES

People get stuck in three areas or "zones" that prevent them from expressing their full magnificence, creativity, and gifts in the world, which we call living in the zone of genius. Gay Hendricks, PhD in his book *The Big Leap*, identifies these four zones.

GENIUS

- What work do you so love doing that it doesn't seem like work?

- Which aspects of your work generate the highest ratio of positive results compared to time spent?

EXCELLENT

- What do you consistently get positive feedback about in your work and life?

- What do you do better than just about anyone else?

INCOMPETENT

- What do you consistently get negative feedback about in your work?

- What work do you do that just about everyone can do better?

COMPETENT

- What work do you do that others can do just as well or better?

- What work do you do well but doesn't feel totally satisfying?

THE ZONE OF INCOMPETENCE. Here, you spend time doing things that you don't enjoy and don't do well. Consider tasks that leave you feeling frustrated, and where someone else could have done a much better job. It's creating a PowerPoint when you don't have the skills, designing your own business cards with no art talent. Or, doing a presentation to your best client with poor public speaking skills and a dread for public presentation. Most organizations won't tolerate people working in their zone of incompetence. However, it still arises regularly in people's home life. It's the time you waste trying to install technology, when you don't have a clue. It's the entire day you spend doing home repairs, when you're not a handy person. It's the hours you work in the kitchen to make homemade Thai food, when take-out tastes better. If it's a dead-end path—if you both dislike like the activity and do it poorly—dump it (stop doing it), delegate it, or do it differently—see if there is a way that you can make it fun. Whichever you choose, exit your zone of incompetence.

The one caveat is if you enjoy tinkering around the house, regardless of the time it takes to do repairs, go for it! If you love playing with spices for hours in the kitchen, regardless of the outcome, continue on the path of enjoyment, play or eventual mastery.

THE ZONE OF COMPETENCE. In this area, you spend time doing things you can do just fine, but others can do them just as well and usually with more efficiency, improved quality, and more enjoyment. These activities might include administrative tasks, like renting a car, finding the cheapest flight, or organizing a corporate party. Or home chores, like mowing the lawn, doing the laundry, or paying bills. The key is a lack of fulfillment and that someone else could do it better. You don't feel that you're wasting time completely, as you do in the zone of incompetence, but at the end of the day, you typically feel unsatisfied and drained. It's like eating a microwave dinner just because it contains adequate caloric content; it has no flavor.

THE ZONE OF EXCELLENCE. This is the trickiest zone, where the majority of successful people get stuck. Here, you are good at what you do. Better than most, in fact. You often receive accolades, prestige, a good paycheck, and many enticing reasons to stay. It's comfortable. It's known. The problem is that it costs you energy: it might be a slight leak, but is a loss of energy nonetheless. The joie de vivre is missing. It feels like work. The passion dies along with your creativity and potential if you stay too long.

UPPER LIMITS. Typically, fear guards the line between the zone of excellence and the ultimate zone of genius. The fears holding people back are many. Who are you to live in your zone of genius? You're not that special. Who can do that? Work is work. Unless you're independently wealthy, you can't just delegate the things you don't want to do. What about your financial responsibilities? That's irresponsible. What if living in your genius means you would choose to abandon others or they would abandon you? What if you just think it's your zone of genius, but it's really just a dream and you fail miserably? It's better to play it safe and stay with what you know. It's just too risky to try.

Hendricks outlines some of the categories of false beliefs that keep us from moving into our zone of genius, calling them the Upper Limits Problem. The big idea is that each of us has a gauge—like a thermostat—that measures how good things are, with a limit just shy of "too good to be true for me." We have a limit for different areas of our lives: how much money we're allowed to make, how much love or closeness we can feel, how much joy we can experience, how much fun we're allowed to have. Everyone's Upper Limits vary, which is why commissioned sales people seem to "top out" at such different numbers. What seems consistent, though, is that when people bump into an Upper Limit, "something happens" that helps bring them back down to a level where they feel safe and comfortable again.

These aren't conscious decisions. You didn't sit down with your coffee this morning and make a deal with yourself to hold your Upper Limits in place: "Hey, self, if we start having too much fun today, let's make sure to have something go wrong (a fight with my boss, a client gets upset, spill something, make an accounting error) to keep things under control."

At the same time, notice all the phrases we casually use in our society:

Too good to be true

Waiting for the other shoe to drop

What goes up must come down

Tallest poppy gets cut

You get what you pay for

> *...fear guards the line between the zone of excellence and the ultimate zone of genius.*

No wonder most people don't expand into their zone of genius. The amount of ease, fun, creativity, and life force often seems "too much."

In addition to the societal reasons, in *The Big Leap*, Hendricks defines four reasons that individuals don't expand into their full magnificence. These are the four top (false) beliefs that trigger the Upper Limits Problem:

Feeling fundamentally flawed. People believe that they cannot expand into their full creative genius because something is inherently wrong with them.

Disloyalty and abandonment. Especially those who have grown up with more humble circumstances believe they cannot experience their full success because it would be disloyal to their roots and they would end up alone.

More success = bigger burden. Those who hold this belief think they can't expand to their highest potential because they will have burdens to handle: more to do, people who want things from them, etc. Life will demand more.

Outshining. Especially for those who are talented or gifted, this belief is that if they expand to their full success, they would outshine someone important to them and make that person look or feel bad.

We contend that these thoughts do not have to be believed and that you can befriend your Upper Limits instead. This involves noticing when you start thinking that something is "too good" so you can teach the nervous system that the feeling or situation is not only possible, but can be the new normal.

Experts say that the nervous system needs to be reprogrammed to allow for greater happiness, fulfillment, and relational connectedness. The good news is that the nervous system is highly receptive to new programming. In fact, it is somewhat capable of reprogramming itself if we provide support. To create the space and allow the nervous system to develop this new capacity, we encourage leaders to integrate just after they experience a new high. For example, you close the deal you never thought you'd be able to close; you get the promotion you've always wanted; you have a great weekend away with your partner and experience a new level of closeness. At these moments, we suggest leaders integrate by doing things that are grounding, ordinary, mindless, soothing, mundane, and/or repetitive. This could be going for a walk, mowing the lawn, sweeping the floor, washing the car, making a meal, flipping through a favorite hobby magazine, or taking a little longer shower. This allows for the gentle raising of old Upper Limits (the reprogramming of the nervous system), without forcefully blowing past them in a way that actually causes a big crash.

THE ULTIMATE ZONE. Commitment 8 says I commit to expressing my full magnificence, and to supporting and inspiring others to fully express their creativity and live in their zone of genius.

When you're in your zone of genius (a.k.a. "flow" or "in the zone"), you spend time doing what you love, what you're uniquely gifted to do. All sense of time disappears. These activities may feel like "nothing" (I would have done that anyway because it's so much fun) yet are often what you get appreciated for. When people are in their zone of genius, we frequently hear them say, "Can't everyone do that easily?" They don't realize that it seems like a Herculean effort to others.

For this reason, genius is difficult to self-identify. It's like telling a fish that it's a genius swimmer. So, using feedback is an important tool to get your genius reflected from others. Because of this, we recommend using an email campaign to many of our clients.

DEVELOPED WITH HENDRICKS.COM

▶ ▶

GENIUS EMAIL EXERCISE

Step 1: Create an email list of 30-50 people who have known you from different areas of your life and for different lengths of time. Include friends, colleagues (past and present), family, and other community members. i.e. (aunts & uncles, college roommates, neighbors who you socialize with, people you share hobbies with, old bosses, teen age children, fellow board members, direct reports, etc.)

Step 2: Create an introductory paragraph similar to the one below. We have learned that our clients get a high ratio of participants when they state a specific time and date to receive responses.

Step 3: Organize the responses by question so you are easily able to see themes.

Step 4: Thank everyone who participated and consider sharing something you have learned from the exercise with them.

Dear community,

I am in the midst of discovering my unique zones of genius (when I'm "in the zone") and would appreciate your help. I am asking for your support by briefly answering a few questions to reflect back to me what you see. If you are willing to offer your input, I request that you respond to the following questions by (give a specific day and time within the next week).

Briefly answer the following questions:

- *What am I doing or talking about when you experience me MOST energized and happy?*

- *When you experience me at my best, the exact thing I am doing is_____. (Fill in the blank)*

- *What do you see as a special skill I am gifted with?*

- *What are your three favorite qualities you see in me? (Do your best to use one word per quality)*

Optional questions to send to participants:

- *What reliably shows up in the room when I do?*

- *How have I most contributed to your life?*

- *What would you miss most about my presence if I passed on?*

▶ ▶

▶ ▶

BEST STUFF EXERCISE

For those committed to living in their zone of genius, we recommend complementing the email campaign with another exercise. Kaley, along with our friend and colleague Jim Warner, created the "Best Stuff" exercise, where you identify Genius Moments. It involves writing down and telling someone, who is skilled at listening for genius, eight stories from your life when you were in the zone—when you loved what you were doing and you did it well. For this exercise, you can't include something you enjoyed but did badly. So the karaoke nights when you had a blast singing, but blasted everyone's ears don't qualify. Similarly, if you excelled at something but didn't enjoy it, leave it out. The award you won for teaching the course you hated is off limits.

You can draw from your entire life for these stories. As Stuart Brown describes in his book *Play*, childhood is often a great place to look. It could be building a birdhouse with your father, training for a race, creating skits with friends, taking pictures, or coaching a team.

Use the Best Stuff sheets provided as a download on our websites to write down your stories. Then look for common themes. This exercise will not tell you to be or do something, but rather, it offers accurate descriptions of where and how you thrive: possible areas of genius.

▶ ▶

For instance, when doing the Best Stuff exercise, one client told story after story of being on stage, performing dramas, sharing stories, and connecting with people. The exercise did not tell her to drop everything and go to Hollywood to be an actress. Instead, she realized that she could bring her love of the stage and drama into her work. She subsequently started a culture initiative in her organization to teach key leadership skills by telling stories and doing dramas.

THE COMMITMENT IN ACTION

A wonderful example of a leader who is living and working in his genius is James Sabry, Sr. Vice President, of Genentech Partnering. James lives in his genius and encourages members of his team to fully express their genius. Rather than seeing his job as a manager to control or direct his team, he has spent time with each person coming to understand and appreciate his or her unique genius qualities. Then, it's James' job to pave the way for them to work and live in their genius. The results have been tremendous.

One of James' employees did an assessment that revealed he had a genius for extended periods of creative and solitary thought. But he struggled to access it in the office environment. He recognized that this creative daydreaming happened more at home, so James trusted him to come in and out of the office as he determined was necessary. James is more devoted to fostering genius than following traditional rules of engagement. This person's (and the team's) creativity has significantly increased.

IN A NUTSHELL

Genius equals juice. The more we live and work in our genius the more the juice of life is flowing through us into the world. As many have said, it is not our failure that we are most afraid of but rather our magnificence. Conscious leaders face the fear of stepping fully into their magnificence. They embrace their magnificence, live and work in their genius and give their gift to the world.

PRACTICING
THE COMMITMENT

Once you know what your zone of genius is, you can start
to shift your calendar to allow more and more time there.

Step 1: Look back over your calendar from the last two weeks
and make a list of 25 activities you performed in the course
of doing your job. Be very specific, e.g. weekly staff meeting,
emailed boss updating him on latest client meeting, filled out
expense report, client meeting with ABC Products, read report
on performance evaluation, had lunch with administrative
assistant, etc.

Put an arrow next to each activity

If your energy went up when you did the activity
put the arrow pointing up

If your energy was flat when you did the activity
make the arrow go horizontal.

If your energy went down when you did the
activity put the arrow pointing down.

Step 2: Look at the amount of time you spent doing each activity
and assign a rough percentage to the amount of time you spent
with energy increasing activities, activities that left your energy
flat, and activities that decreased your energy.

PRACTICING
THE COMMITMENT (CONT)

Would you be willing to have a 10%-20% increase
in energy?

Don't skip over this willingness lightly. Many leaders aren't
willing for the Upper Limit reasons above. If your answer
is yes, then go to the next step.

Step 3: What could you do with activities that drain your energy
(arrow points down) so that you could have more time for
activities that increase your energy?

- *Delegate it*
- *Dump it*
- *Do it differently. Do it in a way that doesn't
  de-energize you.*

Step 4: If you want to spend more time in your zone of genius,
put one of these actions next to each down arrow.

What is your first action step and by when will you do it?

Excelling in your Zone of Genius

► Conscious leaders build an organization that allows all team members to realize their full potential—and they support and inspire others to do the same.

► People tend to work and live in four zones: incompetence, competence, excellence, and genius.

► Conscious leaders are committed to maximizing their zone of genius, where their full magnificence and creativity can be expressed without hesitation.

► Unconscious leaders get stuck in the zones of excellence, competence, and incompetence, never living up to and expressing their extraordinary brilliance.

► The Upper Limits Problem, named by Gay Hendricks, identifies the fears and beliefs that keep people from stepping into their zone of genius.

► We can program our nervous systems to allow for greater happiness, fulfillment, and relational connectedness.

► Becoming aware of our unique giftedness, as well as the environments where that is most valued, (the Best Stuff Exercise) helps us spend more and more of our time thriving.

► Conscious leaders who spend time with team members to assess, understand, and appreciate their own unique genius qualities and talents create organizations that excel on all levels.

Everything is occuring in its perfect timing.

Living a Life of Play and Rest

I commit to creating a life of play,
improvisation, and laughter. I commit to
seeing all of life unfold easefully, and
effortlessly. I commit to maximizing my energy
by honoring rest, renewal, and rhythm.

*I commit to seeing my life as serious; it requires hard
work, effort, and struggle. I see play and rest as
distractions from effectiveness and efficiency.*

Most of us have heard the proverb "All work and no play
makes Jack a dull boy." Few would argue with this wise
philosophy, but when we consider applying it to ourselves,
many of us would debate its validity. After all, we have
bills to pay and deadlines to meet and real work to do.

Many of the business cultures we come across are
committed to a nose-to-the-grindstone mentality.
Employees work long hours, checking their emails and
voicemails throughout their evenings and weekends and
skipping sleep, meals, and physical exercise. They expend
a lot of effort. The number one complaint we hear is that
they lack life balance. They have no time for relaxation,
let alone play, in their professional or personal worlds.

Most of these organizations believe that to stay ahead in the marketplace, they need to work harder than their competition. They have adopted the mindset that equates success with struggle. Bill Gross, the incredibly successful founder and CIO of PIMCO, one of the world's leading asset management firms, was recently asked how PIMCO can continue to succeed and find investments that outperform the markets. His answer, "Hard work." Gross told the audience that he and everyone else at PIMCO works harder than the competition. He said that he still routinely arrives at the office by 4:30 a.m. and is there past 7 PM most nights. Gross is the poster child for great success through tremendously hard work (along with a lot of other great competencies). In many organizations, goals often become more important than quality of life and relationships. It's serious business, and the fear of failure leaves little room for joy and laughter. People in these organizations also report that they have been made to feel guilty for playing or resting, especially when others have chosen to work really hard.

WHAT IS PLAY?

In his book, *Play*, Stuart Brown defines play as "an absorbing, apparently purposeless activity that provides enjoyment and suspends self-consciousness and a sense of time. It is also self-motivating and makes you want to do it again."

We like this definition. From this perspective play is not serious, doesn't require hard work, effort or struggle. The cornerstone of conscious play is that it is not serious.

The best role models for non-serious play are children and animals. The most recent research shows that all mammals are defined (in addition to how they are born) by their love of learning and play. The current best practices approach to training dogs is to use play, even more than food, as a reward for good behavior. Playing ball trumps treats when it comes to what most motivates a dog. Children and animals love to play and they don't take it seriously.

By seriously we mean that they don't make play mean more than it means. They don't make the outcome of play a referendum on their identity or value. They don't "worry" and "stress" about play. At some point in our journey we loose touch with the spirit of play. Life becomes serious. This probably occurs for most of us because our caregivers long ago lost connection with life as play and so they teach us that life and "play" are serious.

We've all witnessed this conflict around play at the soccer field where five year olds who still see play as "apparently purposeless activity that provides enjoyment and suspends self-consciousness and a sense of time" are being chided by parents and coaches to "pay attention, try harder, run faster, FOCUS and WIN." Watching a red-faced adult scream at a child who has chosen to pick a flower on the field and talk to a friend to "PAY ATTENTION AND KICK THE BALL," is all we need to know about how children lose touch with play. As you watch young children who have not yet been fully formed by "serious" caregivers at these moments it's as though they look at the parents and coaches and say, "What are you talking about? I'm just out here playing, having fun, and enjoying the experience in the moment. Why are you making this mean more than it means? You're making it mean something about me and something about you, like whether I'll be able to get a college scholarship for sports and whether you're a good parent."

This is not to say that children playing are not, at times, intensely focused or exerting huge amounts of energy. Of course they are! Many parents have found it nearly impossible to interrupt the focus of a child who is absorbed in play. And how often have we heard adults say that they would give anything to have one tenth of the energy of a child at play? When adults commit to creating a life of play they are often very focused and they exert huge amounts of energy.

But there is a difference between being focused and exerting energy and "hard work, effort and struggle." Hard work, effort and struggle come when: (1) I make meaning out of life and work that causes stress and worry; and (2) I resist and force life rather than cooperate and improvise. For this reason this commitment says, "I commit to creating a life of play, improvisation, and laughter."

The cardinal rule of improvisation is "YES AND." No matter what my fellow creators give me my answer is always "YES AND." In other words I take what is given to me and I adapt, create, and change. This is the great fun and creative juice of improvisation. I can't control what is going to be given to me and as soon as I try to control it, I anticipate, force, effort and struggle, and all possibility of improvisation is sapped from the moment. This is also the source of both the excitement and fear of creative improvisation. In life and work conscious leaders give up trying to control what life is giving them and they step into the fun of YES AND. Together with other collaborators they experience the excitement and fear of the unknown. They experience life.

As a fun field trip take your team and go watch improv or even more powerful, go DO improve while suspending self-consciousness. As you do it ask yourself if you're having fun. Ask yourself if this is the way "work" feels. If your answer to the second question is "no" you're not living this commitment.

Exertion and effort are not the same thing. Effort implies resistance and exertion doesn't. Kaley is an expert skier. Having been raised in Colorado with a family vacation home in Vail she has spent much of her life on the slopes. If you watched her ski a double black diamond mogul run you would see exertion (elevated heart rate, muscles contracting, heavy breathing, sweat covering her body) but you wouldn't see effort. When Kaley skis she doesn't resist the mountain. Most beginners resist the mountain. They effort, struggle and often suffer. Not Kaley. She takes whatever the mountain gives her and flows and improvises her way to playful pleasure.

Conscious leaders do the same. They take whatever life gives them and they improvisationally co-create with others in a spirit of playful pleasure. Often they exert significant energy. They sometimes come to the end of a day physically tired; that good tired that comes from having given it all and left everything on the field. They have been focused, often laser focused but they wouldn't characterize their day as effortful and a struggle and they certainly haven't suffered.

The final test of the first part of this commitment is laughter. Laughter is a key indicator of how much play is going on in a leader and an organization. This laughter is not the typical laughter in many organizations. The humor in most organizations is sarcastic humor that pokes fun at others often when they are not present or sophomoric humor that trivializes what is good and beautiful in life. This kind of humor is actually a sign of unconscious leadership. The laughter being referenced in this commitment is the lighthearted playful laughter that refreshes the soul and is contagious and infectious in its impact. It is a laughter that invites others in and doesn't exclude or cause division. Often this laughter is at ourselves and always comes from love. This kind of laughter changes the physiology of people. It is not only good for the soul but also good for the body and really good for the mind.

STYLES OF PLAY

One thing we notice about play is that people play differently. There is no "right way" to play. Learning your particular style of play and the styles of those around you can be very useful in implementing this commitment. Stuart Brown, in his book *Play*, suggests that people have a dominant mode of play that falls into one of eight play personalities:

THE JOKER: Play always revolves around some sort of nonsense. Making silly sounds with a child or playing a practical joke on a friend fall under this category.

THE KINESTHETE: Those in this group include athletes, dancers, and others who like to push their bodies and feel the result.

THE EXPLORER: These people delight in trying new experiences, such as physically going to new places, emotionally exploring and deepening feelings, and mentally researching or discovering new points of view.

THE COMPETITOR: This person enjoys a competitive game with specific rules and loves fighting for number one!

THE DIRECTOR: These players like planning and executing scenes and events. They are born organizers who give parties and instigate group events.

THE COLLECTOR: This type of player relishes the thrill of having the most and best collection of objects or experiences, such as antiques, cars, or wine.

THE ARTIST/CREATOR: This person's joy comes from making things. Sculpting, woodworking, sewing, and gardening are a few examples. The point is to make something beautiful or functional.

THE STORYTELLER: Here the imagination is the key to the kingdom of play. This group includes novelists, cartoonists, and screenwriters as well as those who like reading stories and watching movies. They are also the performers who use dance, magic, and acting to create an imaginative world.

Consider what styles of play you most enjoy. How do you engage in them and how can you enjoy more play in your life and with your team at work?

For all these styles, the state of being is what's most important. You can do any activity from a place of play or not.

A PLAY BREAK

It is difficult to convince most people that taking time off or resting during the day can actually enhance productivity. Our culture tends to think that the busier we are, the more we will produce. Research from NASA suggests otherwise. They found that organizations whose employees took a nap for at least thirty minutes every day were up to 35% more productive than their competitors. Rest and play are often stored in the same box as behaviors that successful professionals believe they cannot afford to participate in, and yet more and more studies are proving the opposite to be true.

William Duggan's research in *Strategic Intuition: The Creative Spark in Human Achievement* asserts that when you completely let go, of even trying to solve the problem, the brain recategorizes and re-sorts all apparently unrelated information into new innovative solutions. This is the classic example of solving a problem in the shower because new insights are really just new combinations of old ideas that occur during brain states like those during meditation.

Equally impressive, scientists have also determined that people in a relaxed state and good mood are far more likely to develop innovative or creative thoughts. Companies are now taking advantage of this fact. An excellent example is 3M. They have an incredible record of innovation. At 3M, all engineers have an hour a day to do whatever they want, whether that's working on a side project, taking a nap, or tinkering with a hobby. The results speak for themselves. By giving their engineers and product managers a time to relax, 3M's management is actually fostering creativity and moving far beyond just making packing tape.

We recently spoke at the leadership conference of one of the top investment banks in the world, presenting the principles of Conscious Leadership to the senior leaders and their most important clients. Just prior to our talk, author David Rock shared the findings from his fascinating book Your Brain at Work. He discussed the latest science behind how the brain works and how to maximize productivity and effectiveness in the workplace based on this research. These Wall Street leaders are serious about productivity. A question that Rock has asked several thousand leaders over the last few years is how many hours of productive work do you do a day? Answer: about three.

Rock went on to suggest that these leaders' productivity would go up drastically if they understood this and maximized the brain's ability to do great work by prioritizing, eliminating multitasking, checking email later in the morning, taking naps, going for walks, doing creative play projects, and feeling authentic feelings.

We've been back to this investment bank several times since and have yet to see leaders napping on couches, but science supports rest and play as the best way to get the most done for the longest period of time.

The workplace has changed since the 1930s and '40s, when at Henry Ford's River Rouge plant, laughter was a disciplinary offense—and humming, whistling, and smiling were evidence of insubordination. As British management scholar David Collinson recounts,

In 1940 John Gallo was sacked because he was "caught in the act of smiling," after having committed an earlier breach of "laughing with other fellows" and "slowing down the line maybe half a minute." This tight managerial discipline reflected the overall philosophy of Henry Ford, who stated that "When we are at work we ought to work. When we are at play we ought to play. There is no use trying to mix the two." (Daniel Pink, A Whole New Mind, pg 187)

PERSONA PLAY

From the Hendricks Institute, we learned that "persona play" is one the best kinds of play for eliminating struggle and suffering both in ourselves and in our relationships with others. Knowing how best to navigate a vast multitude of situations is a necessary part of life. To do this effectively, we need to develop healthy personas.

Personas are like masks that we wear to present ourselves to others in various circumstances. All of us have many personas, which we can equate to coats hanging in a closet. We can choose a particular persona as we might an outfit to meet the needs of a particular life situation.

When life gets serious and struggle begins, it's likely we did not choose the right persona for the occasion. Instead, we defaulted to a habitual one that we unconsciously believe will help us gain control, security, or approval. You know you are stuck in the grip of a persona when you think, "This is not funny." Sometimes a persona can be very hard to shake off, and play is often the best medicine to loosen its grip and allow the attitude to relax.

Not long ago, we worked with a couple of executives who had been debating for six months over how to restructure their teams. There was no resolution in sight. While they were very politically correct with each other, we sensed an underlying tone of frustration as they defended their points of view. When we began facilitating them, their frustration rose. Neither one had any genuine understanding and appreciation for the other's perspective.

We decided that playing with the issue would likely lead to resolution. We told them to face each other across a table and then take on the attitude of a mob boss. We instructed them to include exaggerated gestures and tone to really ham it up and asked them to go back and forth repeating the saying "Don't mess with my family. No, you don't mess with my family."

They ended up finding a playful way to let off some steam, and their humor began to emerge as they fully recognized their power struggle. Almost immediately, each executive began to appreciate the other's stance, and their curiosity led to an innovative solution they could both align with.

LIST OF POSSIBLE PERSONAS

PROTECTOR	CRITIC	COMPLAINER
PEACEMAKER	REBEL	WORRY WART
ENERGIZER BUNNY	CYNIC	UNAPPRECIATED
FLATTERER	DEBATER	HYPOCHONDRIAC
FIREFIGHTER	CONTROL FREAK	OVERWORKED
CHEERLEADER	GOSSIP	MARTYR
PETER PAN	BULLDOZER	RESIGNED
ANALYZER	DUNCE	OVERWHELMED
SUPERCOMPETENT	TIME COP	MISUNDERSTOOD
MULTITASKER	REPEAT OFFENDER	THE NEEDY ONE
GOOD LISTENER	PURITAN	WHINER
PROVIDER	DRILL SERGEANT	DEPRESSED
WITHDRAWER	MR. SARCASM	DUMMY
GOOD PARENT	KNOW-IT-ALL	THE RELIABLE ONE
NICE GUY	NARCISSIST	LYNCHPIN

DEVELOPED WITH HENDRICKS.COM

MAXIMIZING ENERGY BY HONORING REST, RENEWAL AND RHYTHM

The second part of this commitment is a commitment to maximize energy. We agree with Tony Schwartz and Jim Loehr in their book *The Power of Full Engagement* when they assert that energy management is key to long term effectiveness. In fact, energy management is more important than time management or money management or any other kind of management when in it comes to effective leadership. There are many keys to effective energy management but the one addressed in this commitment is the honoring of natural rhythms. All of creation is a living testimony to honoring the rhythms of life. Conscious leaders become expert in understanding and living by the natural rhythms of their life. This includes the rhythm of the waking state, the dream state and dreamless sleep. Research is showing over and over again the necessity of sleep for high functionality. Many leaders do not understand their natural sleep cycle or honor it. Most ancient traditions embrace the notion of a "sabbath" (a day of rest) as part of the rhythm of the week. Many cultures understood and lived by the seasons and the natural rest that occurred in preparation for the coming of new life.

When we ask leaders to tell us about the rhythms of their life and how honoring those rhythms maximizes their energy we are often greeted with a blank stare. Conscious leaders become expert at knowing how to maximize their energy through all kinds of practices not the least of which is honoring the natural rhythm of life.

WORKAHOLISM

When we talk to leaders and organizations about play we run squarely into the defense mechanism of denial. Denial surfaces, sometimes aggressively but often passive aggressively, when we confront what we consider to be an epidemic of workaholism that permeates our contemporary culture.

From our perspective workaholism is an addiction just like alcoholism, drug addiction, food addiction or sex addiction. The definition we use for addiction is "any behavior we do compulsively (repetitively, with no real experience of freedom to choose another behavior, 'I've got to do it,') in order to avoid experiencing our experience in the moment." Conscious leaders, and for that matter, conscious people, become practiced at living in the now moment and welcoming whatever is being experienced; whatever feelings, sensations and thoughts are arising in the moment are welcomed with no desire to control what is being experienced. This is actually a pretty good definition of consciousness. But many leaders don't welcome what is being experienced. Instead they resist their experience and run from it. For example, when fear or anxiety come up they repress it, deny it and avoid it at all costs. Addictions are behaviors we do repeatedly to run from what is here now. When fear/anxiety are present some leaders run to alcohol, drugs or sex. Others run to television, pornography, eating, shopping, gambling, or exercising (yes, even apparently "good" behaviors can be addictive if we do them to avoid being in the moment with what is happening).

The list of compulsive behaviors goes on and on but at the top of the list for many leaders is work. This work addiction can manifest in many ways, including working excessive hours, destroying any kind of balance and impacting many personal relationships. It can also look like habitually checking our mobile devices, email or texts (sometimes at three in the morning, always first thing in the morning and regularly while we are with loved ones like our children) or compulsive thinking about work that never stops. Alternatively, we see leaders compulsively watching business related TV or reading materials about work. In our experience many leaders work (in all of its many forms including but not limited to those listed above) because they are terrified of being with themselves in this now moment and being with what is arising in them. They don't know how to simply welcome core emotions like fear, anger and sadness. They struggle to be with thoughts without being taken over by thinking or how to feel sensations in their body without numbing them. From our perspective this addiction to work is epidemic in our culture and it is not being faced. There is a collective collusion to live in denial about the reality of our lack of real freedom to choose to do anything other than work.

This commitment on play and honoring the rhythms of life flies headlong into the face of this addiction to work. For this reason, it is one of the commitments leaders push back on the most. Like all addictions, our work addiction must be faced head on if we are to experience the freedom of conscious leadership.

> *...even apparently "good" behaviors can be addictive if we do them to avoid being in the moment with what is happening.*

COMMITMENT IN ACTION

Hopelab Inc. in Redwood City, California, has fully embraced this commitment. Joy is highly valued in their culture, and they frequently create time for play. While playing, they are also generating innovative technology that is changing the lives of thousands of children dealing with life-threatening diseases.

Finding ways to play while disclosing their financial reports at their quarterly meetings was not something they had considered before. The CFO, Dan Cawley, is famous around the office for his impersonation of his mother, who apparently was quite the character with a thick Irish accent. Someone on the team suggested that he present the quarterly financials as if he were his mother. He accepted the invitation and delighted the entire team with his humor while updating them all on the organization's financial status. We heard from Dan's team members that they found themselves more engaged and curious. He was such a hit that there were requests for an encore at future meetings.

We challenge you to experiment with play in your organization. Try it for yourselves and discover how play can support creativity, innovation, and well-being among those you lead. If you are looking for ideas, consider some of the exercises below and please pass along your successes to us.

PRACTICING THE COMMITMENT

When you feel the need to get serious or work much harder, consider doing the following:

- *Take a couple of minutes to argue for why you can't have what you really want.*

- *Make up a country song title that describes your current issue and sing a line.*

- *Have a fifteen-second temper tantrum. Be sure to include your whole body and make noise.*

- *For thirty seconds, hop on one foot and flap your arms as you discuss your serious issue.*

- *Radically (and we mean RADICALLY) change your current body posture and then talk about your issue for one minute.*

- *Sing "I am right—you are wrong" to the tune of your favorite nursery rhyme.*

DEVELOPED WITH HENDRICKS.COM

IN A NUTSHELL

Possibly nothing we teach is more mysterious, more resisted and more transformational and healing than the commitment to play and to maximize energy through honoring the rhythms of life. This is one of the great lessons children have to teach all leaders committed to consciousness. They are masters of this commitment and beneficiaries of its gifts.

Living a Life of Play and Rest

- ▶ Creating a life of play, improvisation, and laughter allows life to unfold easily and energy to be maximized.

- ▶ Play is an absorbing, apparently purposeless activity that provides enjoyment and suspends self-consciousness and a sense of time. It is also self-motivating and makes you want to do it again.

- ▶ An imposed nose-to-the-grindstone culture will lead to higher levels of stress, guilt, employee burnout and turnover.

- ▶ Energy exerted with this type of "hard work" is wrought with effort and struggle, whereas energy exerted through play is energizing.

- ▶ Most leaders resist play because they think they will fall behind if they aren't seriously working hard.

- ▶ Organizations that take breaks to rest and play are actually more productive and creative. Energy is maximized when rest, renewal, and personal rhythms are honored.

- ▶ Conscious leaders who value and encourage an atmosphere of play and joy within themselves and in their organizations create high-functioning, high-achieving cultures.

- ▶ Workaholism is just like any other addiction, and it is an epidemic in the corporate world.

"One point of view is too small for the whole truth" -unknown

COMMITMENT TEN

Exploring the Opposite

I commit to seeing that the opposite of my story is as true as or truer than my original story. I recognize that I interpret the world around me and give my stories meaning.

*I commit to believing my stories and
the meaning I give them as the truth.*

Jim Barnett, the founder and CEO of Turn Inc., a tech company in Silicon Valley, no longer enjoyed leading his organization. He cared deeply for the company and his teams and wanted what was in the best interest of everyone. When we first met him, he firmly believed that a founder should stay for a certain time or risk damaging the organization. This belief caused him a lot of suffering because his heart was no longer in the role and yet his mind was unwilling to consider leaving as a viable option.

Almost all the challenges we see businesses struggle with arise from people believing they are right about the way they perceive situations, one another, or themselves. To understand this, pick an issue that you are wrestling with in your life. When you look underneath, can you see your desire to be right about that issue? For example, you need

to be right about the way your field team communicates with the home office. Or, you need to be right about the way your five-year-old shares with her playmates. What else do you need to be right about?

If you're having trouble finding something, just look for any complaint or judgment. At the root of both of these, there is something you think you are right about.

Do you see that having to be right is making you suffer? To call it suffering may seem dramatic but in our experience those who look closely at the experience of believing their thoughts find some form of suffering. Whenever we don't allow reality to be what it is, we are in opposition to life. This opposition is the cause of all suffering. For example, when we don't allow the field team to communicate as it does, we find ourselves agitated; wanting to change the way that team is acting. This agitation and our desire to change what is so, is a form of suffering. When we don't accept the reality of how our five year old is playing with her friends—when there is a right way to play with children—our suffering occurs in the experience of being separate from our child. And in wanting to force her to be something other than who she is. The overarching truth is that whenever you don't accept the suchness of life, suffering occurs.

It is actually not the issue that causes the pain but your interpretation of it. Life doesn't come with labels. It just comes. We give life the labels. And the label that we give life determines how we experience it. For example, let's take a big topic. Death doesn't come with a label. But people have very different experiences of the idea of death. Some people give it a label of terror: this is the end of all there is; this is the ultimate loss and separation. Others give death a label of freedom: it's a place of deliverance and redemption. Others look at death and give it no label whatsoever. It's just the next occurrence, neither positive nor negative. Death itself doesn't have a label, but the label we give it determines our experience of it.

On a more lighthearted note, there were three umpires talking. The first said, "There are balls and strikes and I call them as they are." The second said, "There are balls and strikes and I call them as I see them." The third said, "There are only pitches until I call them." For our purposes, the first one believes things have a label and his job is to get the label right. The second believes that things have a label and his interpretation of the label is important. The third doesn't think anything has a label until he assigns it one. We agree with the third umpire: life doesn't have a label until we give it one.

Conscious leaders take responsibility for being the labeler of life. They learn to question all of the labels.

Having trouble with this idea? You're not alone. Commitment 10 challenges the part of us that really wants to hold on to being right, which propels us into the drama triangle. Wanting to be right is the compulsion of the ego. In fact, the ego believes that unless it is right, it cannot survive. So the mind is addicted to believing that there is a right way to be.

IS YOUR STORY TRUE?

In his book *The Happiness Hypothesis*, Jonathon Haidt, former associate professor of psychology at the University of Virginia, suggests that one of the keys to happiness is using reframing to challenge our automatic, stressful thoughts. His research shows that if we are willing to reframe our subjective perspective, we can feel a sense of well-being in a matter of minutes. This practice requires us to let go of being right and get deeply curious about how we see ourselves and the world around us.

Reframing comes in many forms, and one of our favorites is *The Work* of Byron Katie. In 1986 Katie, now an author and speaker, from the depths of a ten-year-long depression, experienced a life-changing realization:

I discovered that when I believed my thoughts, I suffered, but that when I didn't believe them, I didn't suffer, and that this is true for every human being. Freedom is as simple as that. I found that suffering is optional. I found a joy within me that has never disappeared, not for a single moment. That joy is in everyone, always.

She created a simple way to help herself and others examine the beliefs that cause suffering. This tool invites

us to ask four questions about a stressful thought.
The purpose is to help us find our own truth.

- *Is it true?*
- *Can you absolutely know that it's true?*
- *How do you react, what happens, when you
  believe that thought?*
- *Who would you be without the thought?*

The follow-up step to these four questions, the
"turnaround," allows us to experience various
opposites of the original thought.

Let's take our example from the opening of the chapter
and show you how Jim used *The Work* to eliminate his
struggles and create alignment in his life. The thought
that made him suffer was "I am irresponsible if I leave
my role as CEO."

We first asked, "Is it true?" And he quickly responded
yes. He believed he was right about this thought.

"Can you absolutely know that it's true?" we questioned.
He paused, got curious, and said that he could not
absolutely know that it was true. We have never met a
genuinely curious person who claims that she can know
unequivocally that a judgment of hers is absolutely true.

Next, we inquired, "How do you react when you believe
that thought?" Jim said he felt frustrated, scared, and sad,
and felt trapped.

> *...if we are willing to reframe our subjective perspective, we can feel a sense of well-being in a matter of minutes.*

With this next question, we asked him to close his eyes and relax his breath: "Who would you be without the thought?" He wasn't exactly sure what we meant, so we invited him to consider that his brain was like a computer and his thought like a software program. "What if for the next few minutes, we could erase that software program so it didn't exist anywhere in your brain—who would you be then?"

He took a few breaths to actually allow himself to discover what was occurring for him in the moment without the thought. Jim reported that he was experiencing a sense of both freedom and peace. His breath began to expand and we noticed a softening around his eyes. He was present, not just in his head, but also in his body. Nothing about his life had changed except his thinking.

Not everyone experiences this presence doing this exercise. Some will still find that their mind is unwilling to let go of being right. If this happens for you, Katie says, "it's because you are not answering the questions of *The Work*; you are justifying or defending the thoughts you began the process with. When you are truly open to questioning your stressful thoughts, the thoughts will let go of you. Would you rather be right or free?"

▶ ▶

THE TURNAROUND

More "ahas" are discovered during the final, turnaround step, when you have an opportunity to experience the opposite of what you believe to be true. The idea here is to see that the opposite of your story is at least as true as, if not truer than, your original thought. These realizations can set you free and create lasting shifts in your thinking and perception of yourself and the world around you.

Example: John is unkind to me.

Turn it around to the opposite: John is kind to me.

Turn it around to the other person: I am unkind to John.

Turn it around to yourself: I am unkind to me.

How is this statement as true or truer? (For "I am unkind to me," exactly how have you been unkind to yourself in this situation? In other situations?) Give at least three specific, genuine examples.

Find a minimum of three examples in your life where each turnaround is true.

Circling back to our work with Jim, we took his original judgment—"I am irresponsible if I leave my role as CEO"—and turned it around to the statement "I am responsible if I leave my role as CEO."

We asked him if he could see how that statement was true. His first thought was that his heart was no longer in the role. While he had the talent, he was concerned that his lack of passion would affect his ability to lead. Leaving his role would open the space for someone else to step in and provide that needed passion.

He also recognized that staying as CEO out of duty was causing him stress and affecting his health. Leaving the role would support his health, which he believed was a responsible act, not only for his well-being, but also for the best interest of his family and organization.

Finally, Jim recognized that if he made the change, he would have the time and space to get aligned with his core purpose and design a legacy to give his life meaning. All three of these examples helped him understand that he could be as responsible leaving the role as staying, if not more so.

We also explored how the following statements were equally as true as his original judgment.

I am irresponsible if I leave my role as CEO.

I am irresponsible if I stay in my role as CEO.

Jim now understood that his original thought was arguable and therefore could no longer believe he was right. As he let go of his certainty, he started to get curious and relaxed into his innate intelligence. He made the choice to step down as CEO and found a leader he believed was better suited to move the organization forward. The company continues to thrive, and Jim enjoys his involvement as the head of the board of directors.

▶ ▶

The purpose of *The Work* is to become curious about all the possibilities of life. We find that this is done most effectively if you remain unattached to any outcome. This is not about valuing one thought above another, but staying truly open to the exploration.

PRACTICING
THE COMMITMENT

We find the resources from Byron Katie to be invaluable in this process. Her website **www.thework.com** has examples, videos, and Worksheets for the practice of questioning thoughts. We recommend watching the videos of Katie doing The Work with participants to have the experience and really "get it."

IN A NUTSHELL

When we let go of the righteousness of our beliefs that drive us to live in the drama triangle, we open to curiosity and align with our deepest desires. We live our lives free of "shoulds" and "have tos" and enjoy both great freedom and peace.

CHAPTER SUMMARY
Exploring the Opposite

▶ Exploring the opposite means being open to the notion that the opposite of your story (thoughts, beliefs, opinions) could be as true as or truer than your story.

▶ It is not the issue itself that causes pain, but your interpretation of it.

▶ Conscious leaders take responsibility for being the labeler of their experiences and their life, and they learn to question all their labels.

▶ The Work of Byron Katie (**www.thework.com**) is a powerful tool in learning how to question beliefs that could likely be holding us back.

▶ Conscious leaders practice simple ways to question the beliefs that cause suffering, starting with "Is it true?" and "Can I absolutely know it is true?"

▶ The turnaround exercise allows leaders to practice shifting their beliefs from knowing to curiosity.

▶ When conscious leaders let go of the righteousness of their beliefs, they open to curiosity and align with their deepest desires.

Sourcing Approval, Control and Security

I commit to being the source of my approval, control and security.

I commit to living from the belief that my approval, control, and security come from the outside - from people, circumstances, and conditions.

Humans have three core wants: approval, control, and security. All other "wants" stem from these basic desires, whether it's wanting success, a raise, fame, a new car, healthy children, a unified leadership team, greater profitability, or dependable coworkers. Wants come in both big and small packages, from wanting my office to be two degrees cooler right now to wanting to live a life of significance. The point of this chapter is that all wants, regardless of their size, are actually just three core wants showing up in a multitude of manifestations.

For example, Jeff is one of our coaching clients. He is renowned as one of the best investment professionals in the world. He is a household name for those who read financial publications or watch CNBC. A recent coaching call began as many do with us asking the question,

"What's currently got your attention?" Jeff responded with the following. "This moment what has my attention is:"

- *I'm angry that an I.T. initiative we have around portfolio construction is way behind schedule.*

- *Our legal department didn't get the filings done for a new fund so we won't be able to launch this year.*

- *My teenager is doing poorly at boarding school and I don't think she is going to pass this semester.*

- *I'm still not exercising and I'm fat.*

- *One of our portfolio managers isn't really living our cultural values and I think he might need to go.*

- *My wife asked her mother to join us on our trip to Paris next month and I'm pissed.*

All of these issues are really wants (as most issues are):

- *I want a better portfolio construction system automated by I.T.*

- *I want this fund launched this year.*

- *I want my kid to succeed in school.*

- *I want to be fit.*

- *I want our leaders to live our values.*

- *I want to be on vacation with my wife alone.*

All of our complaints, desires, dreams, issues, plans, goals, worries, etc. are simply "wants." Leaders and all people want a lot. Commitment 11 begins by identifying that all of these apparently disparate wants come from wanting approval, control and security.

Validation Station

Powerful
Attractive
Good
Important

Good for 1hr of self-esteem.

THREE CORE WANTS: APPROVAL, CONTROL, AND SECURITY

The wanting of security is the most basic of the core desires. At its root, wanting security is wanting to survive. Another word for security is safety. Most of us believe we are a separate self that has a beginning and an end (birth and death), and therefore we do everything we can to make sure this separate self survives. We want to survive physically, to live and not to die. From this deepest want for physical survival comes the desire for security. We want financial security, occupational security, material security, relational security. This wanting of security, survival and safety is core to every human being.

The second core want is approval. Approval is the desire to be loved, liked, wanted, valued, appreciated, respected, to belong, and to be part of something. The desire for approval comes from the desire to survive. Quite simply, at its most evolutionary core, if others approve of me they won't kill me. Since survival is my deepest desire then my strategy for survival is to gain approval.

The third core want is control. If I can't gain security through approval then I'll get it through control. If I can't earn your approval, then I'll try to control you and life. Wanting control is trying to make sure that everything in life goes the way I want. I try to control myself, people, circumstances, God, and everything else. I invest significant energy in my control plan.

Our belief is that these three core wants are underneath all other wants. Let's look again at Jeff and his wants and see if we can identify the possible core wants that give rise to a few of his "surface" desires.

I want this fund launched this year.

- *I need a three-year track record, which determines my success in this industry (Security).*

- *I want to know that when I ask departments to do something, they do it—I want to control the behaviors of the team members in my organization (Control).*

- *I want Wall Street to respect me (Approval).*

I want my kid to succeed in school.

- *I'm concerned for my child's security, and therefore mine if she can't take care of herself (Security).*

- *What will other people think of me (Approval)?*

- *I want to limit my child's suffering, and my suffering if she doesn't succeed (Control).*

I want to be fit.

- *I don't want to die early (Security).*

- *I want to look good (Approval).*

- *I want to control what I eat and how much my body moves (Control).*

Conscious leaders regularly ask themselves, "What is the core want driving this (surface) desire?"

IS IT OUT THERE?

Most leaders and most people believe and are deeply committed to the belief that what they want (approval, control and security) is "out there." Out-there-ness is the belief that my approval, control and security are dependent on someone or something other than myself. Put simply, I don't have it within me and something or someone needs to give it to me. Out-there-ness leads to "if-only-ness." If only my boss would appreciate me, then I would have the sense of approval I so desperately want. If only I had an employment contract, I would have the security that I need. If only my child would obey me I would be in control. Unconscious leaders are in the trance of "out-there-ness" and "if-only-ness." They are driven by them.

One thing we highly recommend for leaders who desire to wake up out of this common trance is to identify how out-there-ness and if-only-ness are showing up in their life. This can be done by simply completing this sentence over and over:

"If only _____ would _____
I would have approval/control/security."

You can start by simply making a list of things in your life you wish were different. Once you have the list look underneath the issue and find the "if only" and the "other-ness" and see which want is at the center of the issue. For example:

- *If only I would lose weight, I would have approval and security.*

- *If only I would quit making stupid mistakes, I would have control and approval.*

- *If only my clients would take time to listen to my presentation, I would have approval and security.*

- *If only my husband would stop drinking so much, I would have control.*

- *If only the President would deliver on his promises, I would have security.*

- *If only my boss would give me a bonus, I would have security.*

Just a quick comment as you begin this exercise. Many people we coach through this process ask about happiness. They think that what they really want is happiness, that happiness is the core want. What we have learned is that happiness for most people is a result of feeling that they have approval, control and security. Our advice is to go below the desire for happiness and see which of the core wants is missing.

According to Commitment 11 one thing that distinguishes conscious from unconscious leaders is where they are looking to meet their deepest needs: out there or in here? But, there is more.

"WANTING" IS THE ISSUE, NOT THE WANTS

When we first explain this concept to leaders a common response is this, "So, are you saying that there is something wrong with approval, control and security? Because if you are I don't get it. These things are what my life is about." Our answer is simple, there is nothing wrong with approval, control and security. In fact they are part of the life of every person and every leader.

The issue is "wanting" approval, control and security. As soon as we want something, anything, it implies that we don't have it. Wanting comes from a belief in lack. I can only want what I believe I don't already have. Wanting approval, control and security implies that I don't already have them. Wanting says I don't have it and I need to go outside of myself to get it. This belief in lack can be found at the root of all suffering and the cause of all seeking. Leaders who believe they lack approval, control and security are always trying to get them from someone or something on the outside.

If I don't believe I have security, I'll try to get it by increasing my net worth or by looking for investments that have little risk or by working hard to guarantee my physical survival. I'll do everything I can to hold on to my job/career because I believe that the key to my security is having my job. I'll put in sophisticated alarm systems on my house and carry weapons and always be looking over my shoulder for any and all threats to my survival.

If I don't believe I have approval, then I'm always seeking approval from people around me. I believe that if my spouse would love me the way I want to be loved then I would have approval. I seek approval from my boss, my board, my clients, my children, my parents, my neighbors and most importantly from myself. I seek it because I don't believe I have it and I've got to go get it from someone or something.

When I believe I lack control, then I'm always seeking to control people, circumstances and myself. I try to control how people act, what they believe, how they relate to me and others. I try to control my thoughts, desires and impulses. I invest huge amounts of energy in controlling myself and others.

Again, this is just what people do. Because they believe they lack core needs (approval, control, security) they want to get them. This wanting leads to all kinds of beliefs and behaviors that are counter to conscious leadership. This entire "game" is unconscious. It is the operating system of the ego and in the background for leaders and their teams. With this commitment we invite leaders to make conscious their compulsion to want, their belief that they are lacking. We invite leaders to see the pattern. Once seen, a leader has a choice.

WHAT IF I ALREADY HAVE APPROVAL, CONTROL, AND SECURITY?

One of our mentors and the person who introduced us to this paradigm around "wants" is Hale Dwoskin. Hale is the teacher of the Sedona Method, a very simple technique for dealing with wanting and the suffering and seeking that comes from a belief in lack. One of our favorite quotes from Hale is, "You cannot go anywhere to get what you already have and you cannot do anything to become what you already are." This is a game changer! What if you already have security, control and approval? What if what you are is already totally secure and safe and its survival is already guaranteed? What if you already are totally approved of, loved, accepted, wanted and valued just as you are? What if everything that is worth being controlled is already completely under your control? If all of the above is true then the vast majority of human effort is a waste of time. Most leaders spend most of their time living in fear that they lack approval, control and security. They then act from this fear to try to get it. What if you already have it now? Wow.

In an oversimplified way, all leaders at any moment are operating from one of two beliefs/experiences: those who believe they lack something and want it and are seeking to get it from someone or something outside of themselves, and those who believe they are already whole, perfect, and complete and lack nothing. These leaders move in the world from a very different energy. Those who believe they lack move in the world from fear and those who believe they are already whole, perfect, and complete, lacking nothing, move in the world from love and creativity.

COMMITMENT IN ACTION

Brian, is a member of the Conscious Leadership Group. He is also the founder and COO of a commercial bakery supplying products to leading food retailers around the world. His company is not just a job or career for Brian. It's a passion. And like many entrepreneurial passions, this one was forged through a partnership.

In the mid 1980's Brian met the man who would become his business partner and his best friend. In 1991 Brian and Andy started with a $200 investment that grew to a $95 million enterprise. What a ride! In 2009 the business and partnership began to fray when a key customer pulled out and $38 million in revenue went away overnight. Under the financial pressure, Brian and Andy began to have different visions for the business and the business culture. This lack of alignment caused a serious rift in their relationship, and tension and conflict became the norm. What was once a creative partnership and a deep friendship turned into a toxic mess.

Many who are reading this book have experienced the loss of a dream and many more have experienced the loss of a great relationship. Brian experienced both. In recent years the business has come back but the relationship between Brian and Andy hasn't. The loss of his relationship with Andy has affected him profoundly in his wanting of approval, control, and security. This effect has not been a one-time blow to Brian's identity but rather a sustained experience of pain and loss.

During the entire process Brian has practiced the six-step process outlined below (and other versions of it). By practice we mean that he has spent hours and hours "letting go" of his "wanting" of approval, control and security and experiencing that even in the midst of

> *Those who believe they lack move in the world from fear and those who believe they are already whole, perfect, and complete, lacking nothing, move in the world from love and creativity.*

profound disappointment and pain he can experience deep peace and equanimity. From Brian's experience this process works and he has learned to reliably source approval, control, and security from the inside.

Let us be clear. Sourcing approval, control, and security from the inside does not mean that we can escape pain. When life happens, bodies and hearts can break. Pain in life is not optional, but suffering is. As long as we keep seeking and wanting something we believe we don't have we suffer. Once we experience the approval, control, and security that is, we can move through the ups and downs of life with peace, joy, and love and not "at the effect of" outward circumstances.

PRACTICING
THE COMMITMENT

One of the things we do with leaders we coach is invite them to explore both their beliefs and their actual experience. This process takes many forms but a very simple starting point comes from the Sedona Method. It works by asking yourself these questions:

At any moment (especially when you are upset and stressed) ask yourself *"What do I want?"* Don't try to edit your answer or be mature about it. Just blurt.

Ask yourself, *"Could I welcome this wanting? Could I simply allow this wanting to be here just as it is?"*

Ask yourself, *"If I dig a little deeper, is this desire coming from wanting approval, control or security?"* (The key to this is to answer from your heart not your head. You can't be wrong about your answer and if you're not sure just pick one.)

Ask yourself, *"Could I welcome this wanting? Could I just allow it to be here?"*

Ask yourself, *"Could I let this wanting go, just for now, just in this moment as best I could?"*

Ask yourself, *"Could I rest for this moment as that (someone) which is beyond all wanting?"*

In our experience this six-step process is totally transformative and unbelievably simple. For many of the leaders we know this process has become for them a regular practice that they choose several times a day. This is a practice of conscious leaders.

IN A NUTSHELL

What if everything in this moment in your life is actually whole, perfect and complete? What if you are lacking nothing? Not just what if you believed you lacked nothing (which is a mind game) but what if your actual experience in this moment was that nothing was missing? How would you be? This commitment suggests that there is nothing missing—no lack—and that conscious leaders experience this moment by moment as they live and lead in the world.

CHAPTER SUMMARY

Sourcing Approval,
Control and Security

► Humans have core wants of approval, control, and security. All other wants are versions of these three basic desires, which show up in a multitude of ways.

► Security is about survival, approval is about belonging and being part of something, and control is the ego's last resort if it cannot achieve security through approval.

► The challenge is not in having approval, control, and security, but in believing that they are missing. This causes people to seek these core desires outside themselves—somewhere "out there."

► The "If Only . . . I Would" exercise can help leaders wake up from the trance that their happiness is located outside themselves.

- ▶ It's not the wants but the "wanting" of something different that leads to an unsatisfying life.

- ▶ The Sedona Method (**www.sedona.com**) offers questions and practices to source security, approval, and control from within.

- ▶ All leaders at any moment are operating from one of two experiences: either they think they lack something and seek to get it from somewhere or someone, or they believe they are already whole, perfect, and complete and move in the world from love and creativity.

COMMITMENT TWELVE

Having Enough of Everything

I commit to experiencing that I have enough
of everything... including time, money, love,
energy, space, resources, etc.

---

*I commit to a scarcity mentality choosing to see
that there is "not enough" for me and others in
the world and therefore I have to be conscious of
making sure I get and preserve what is "mine."*

We find that when we share the commitments of conscious
leadership with the individuals we work with and coach,
regularly the commitment to sufficiency rather than
scarcity arises as one of the most challenging. Most people
have been trained by their parents, school and society that
there are haves and have-nots, and it's better to be one than
the other. The beliefs about scarcity attach to all sorts of
topics: time, money, energy... but really this commitment
is not an exploration of each individual area, but the
mentality that supports the experience of enough—or not.

SCARCITY

In July 2010, we gathered in Chicago for a Conscious
Leadership "playdate." Having previously attended a
Foundation retreat, participants were committed to

a deeper exploration of conscious leadership. We focused on shifting our scarcity beliefs—and those beliefs were plentiful.

"I don't have enough time," people said. "I'm the CEO of a company, plus I have kids. I'm not sure how to balance it all. I feel like I'm constantly falling behind, not doing something well, and running out of time. I understand all about efficiency and schedules—I don't know who watches TV, but it's certainly not me!"

"I don't have enough money," others lamented. "I need to keep working hard—sometimes at the expense of my own natural rhythm or balance to make sure there's enough. College, the mortgage, saving for retirement... it all adds up really quickly. Plus, what if—heaven forbid—something happens?"

"I don't get enough from my relationship," reported some. "Sexually, it's not fulfilling and we aren't deeply connected as friends anymore. Many times we're good co-parents, but it doesn't feel like there's enough love for the kids and me. If my partner loved me enough, I wouldn't feel so lonely—or like I needed to earn his or her love through my actions." Others recognized themselves on the other side: "I don't give enough to my relationship," they shared with a sense of sadness. "I don't have enough energy to give to everyone who wants attention from me."

In addition to these themes, people experience momentary scarcity. For example, it's raining right now and I want to go for a walk—a scarcity of sunlight and dryness. On the other hand, it was a hot summer (ninety to a hundred degrees every day)—with a scarcity of rain and cool temperatures. It's time for breakfast and the homemade granola is almost gone. I am visiting my in-laws and have no time for myself. Yet just last week, my family was gone and I didn't have enough company. I have young kids and don't sleep enough, resulting in a lack of energy (which I attempt to remedy with caffeine).

Lynne Twist is an expert on scarcity and abundance relationships that different cultures have with money. She describes in her book The Soul of Money, "This mantra of not enough carries the day and becomes a kind of default setting for our thinking about everything... [and] grows into the great justification for an unfulfilled life. It becomes the reason we can't have what we want or be who we want to be. It becomes the reason we can't accomplish the goals we set for ourselves, the reason our dreams can't come true, or the reason other people disappoint us, the reason we compromise our integrity, give up on ourselves or write off others."

Are you an entrepreneur suffering from a lack of interest around your idea, or an established business leader struggling with too few opportunities for growth? Perhaps you are succeeding in a business sense, but don't have enough time to do it all. All these scarcity stories keep you at the effect of whichever resource you deem scarce. The stories of scarcity are so prevalent that rather than tell you more stories of others, we encourage you to look at your own life and experiences. Where are you living from the belief that you don't have enough?

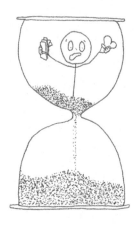

TOXIC MYTHS

Lynne Twist identified three toxic myths of scarcity. The first is that there is never enough. It generates a fear that drives us to make sure we're not the ones left out. The second myth is that more is better. The primary cost of this belief is that it never allows us to arrive—we are always pursuing something more. The final myth is that's just the way it is: it's a hopeless, helpless, unequal, unfair world that we can never change or escape. As Twist argues, this is one of the most challenging myths because the less willing that people are to question beliefs about scarcity, the more entrenched the culture of scarcity becomes.

SCARCITY AND COMPARISON

With these myths as a foundation, we can easily see how scarcity requires a comparison of some sort. The comparison might involve another person: your neighbor has more money than you do or has more energy. Or it might involve an abstract ideal: you thought you'd have enough money to retire when you reached fifty, but you're fifty now and you'd feel unsafe retiring with your current assets.

The "more is better" myth extends far beyond just money. It is also better to have more than less time. It is better to have more resources, a bigger house, and a healthier family. Even as a country, we value how many natural resources we have and assert that more is better. We discovered a new source of natural gas—we're better off now than when we didn't have it. Giving a better life to our kids is correlated with providing "more" for them than we had: a more expensive education, more opportunities, more support. This "more is better" assumption is so engrained, and so popularized, that very few people challenge it.

We have found that whenever people experience life from the perspective of "not enough," what immediately follows is competition. When there is not enough for everyone, we need to make sure that we don't end up with the short end of the stick. This cascades such that resources seem personal. We believe that time is "ours" to control and that energy is something we are allocated. We accuse others of wasting "our" time and draining "our" energy. Because these resources are precious, each of us must fight for our share.

Depending on the person you ask, many of our clients could be viewed as living with much more than they need. Ask any one of the billion women living on between two and five dollars a day whether the three-hundred-thousand-dollar bonus payment was "enough" to compensate for the extra business brought to the firm and the question starts to sound silly.

Rather than getting bogged down in First and Third World comparisons, conduct your own self-inquiry. Whom do you compare yourself against? Your neighbors? Your college friends? Others in your company? People in the news? On TV? How do you judge yourself when you make these comparisons? Do you see yourself as better than or less than? As having more or fewer resources? What beliefs and experiences come up for you?

SCARCITY IN THE WORKPLACE

We once worked with a wealth management company that had just been acquired by a bank. The bankers and the development officers were supposed to team together to increase "wallet share," the amount of a person's net worth that they held. The new organization didn't recognize the synergies that were supposed to occur. Instead, bankers hoarded their clients, afraid that they would be "poached" by the development officers. In turn, the development officers went to valued referral sources and tried to direct all new business to them instead of to the bankers. Distrust was rampant; competition was brutal. They believed that there were not "enough" clients to go around. They had to fight with one another for clients. And even more, they had to protect the clients they had. Now it was not just the external threats of other entities, it was internal. Information protection became the new norm. From the scarcity mindset held by these professionals, each person needed to fight to get what he needed, and once he had it, he needed to protect it from others.

We quickly noticed the myths of scarcity at work in one of our client firms: the beliefs that there wasn't enough, that more was better, and that there was nothing they could do about it. Maybe these conscious principles worked in nonprofit organizations, they said, but in financial services, it couldn't be any other way.

I commit to living from the belief that I have enough of everything... including time, money, love, energy, space, resources, etc.

The unraveling of the scarcity belief begins as soon as we adopt a different reference point. Taking on a global perspective, we can acknowledge that there actually is enough for all of us. There is enough food in the world for no one to go hungry. When we change our belief to one of sufficiency—when we believe we have enough of everything—our experience of the same situation changes. Lynne Twist reminds us, though, that sufficiency isn't an amount. It's not comparative at all. Instead, sufficiency is "an experience, a context we generate, a declaration, a knowing that there is enough and we are enough."

PERSPECTIVE MATTERS

Rather than getting sucked into comparing your perspective with others', consider that your own perspective matters. For example, we often hear people comment that they don't have enough time. This is a great place to see how your perspective matters. Think of a time when you were exercising and every second seemed to last for hours. In contrast, think of a conversation with a close friend when the time flew by and an hour felt like minutes. As an illustration, we conducted an experiment to study these opposing perceptions: we asked one person to spend five minutes meditating and another to spend the same amount of time holding a cinder block straight out in front of him. As you can imagine, the two people experienced time quite differently! The "same" amount of time shifts based on our perspective: whether we want something to be over or last longer.

Gay Hendricks writes extensively about the shifting view of time in his book *The Big Leap*. Hendricks differentiates between the linear, constant Newtonian Time and the elastic Einstein Time, which expands to allow extra creative output, experience, or connection in the same amount of minutes. If you're interested in enjoying abundant time, we encourage you to read Hendricks.

In a similar exploration of how your vantage point determines whether there is sufficiency or lack, we also encourage you to look at money from various perspectives. When you were just out of college, what was your income? What was life like when you had that amount of money? Many people tell us stories of the freedom they experienced when they had "less" and yet it was enough for their life. A CEO who works and travels constantly now reminisces about the time in his life when he had just enough money for his bar bill and greens fees—and life was good. Shift your perspective and imagine having that same amount of money now. What does it feel like?

THE EXPERIENCE OF ENOUGH

For some, especially those in the world of business, this concept can seem too abstract or aspirational. Our experience matches that of Lynne Twist, "business and entrepreneurial energy grounded in the principles of sufficiency leads to success and sustainable growth, while... business rooted in scarcity only creates financial

instability and eventually proves unsustainable, even if
the short-term gains seem highly profitable." She goes
on to explain the three truths of sufficiency: (1) money
is like water—regardless of the flow, you direct where
it goes; (2) what you appreciate, appreciates; and (3)
collaboration creates prosperity. We highly recommend
The Soul of Money for an in-depth exploration of how
to run a business (and experience life) from the starting
point of sufficiency.

▶ ▶

THE SUFFICIENCY MEDITATION

To experience the shift from scarcity to sufficiency in this
moment—since sufficiency is a state of being, not just a
data point—we recommend doing this meditation:

**Check in this moment to see what your experience is
right now.** In this moment, allow yourself to take a few
deep breaths. Notice the air moving in and out of your
lungs. And notice the breath that sustains you. And that
there is enough.

And bring your attention to your physical body. Pay
attention to any sensations. Notice what is. See if there is
anything lacking. Check to see in this moment right now
what your experience is. As you breathe in, notice the
wholeness of your physicality.

In this moment now, notice your experience of time.
Notice that there is no past and no future. There is only
now. The past is behind and the future is ahead. In this

now moment, what is your relationship with time? Notice that the edges of time begin to blur as now refreshes itself with each moment. Always now. And check to see in this now moment if you have enough time.

As you continue this exercise, bring to your mind anything that you have been believing is scarce, that you don't have enough of. And check in this now moment if anything is missing. Or if you have everything you need, neither excess nor scarcity.

Notice that when you are fully present in this now moment, you have plenty of everything. Everything is perfect. Because it just is. To experience scarcity, you must be outside yourself and the present moment—anticipating the lack of something in the future or harboring the lack of something from the past. When there is just now, there is always enough.

Let's revisit our financial services merger. While still not perfect, the culture of this team's interaction changed when we spent time with them. As a thought experiment, we wondered what would happen if they believed that there were plenty of clients for everyone and that they would not only keep their jobs, but also have more business than they could handle alone. The group was able to look together at the pool of potential clients and shift their perspective. They saw that they actually offered complementary services. Solutions that had previously seemed impossible became obvious. The bankers could provide lending resources and the development officers could invest their assets. By partnering with each other instead of protecting their turf, they enjoyed more opportunities to do business with their ideal target clients. Those clients got a better experience, and the company's profits increased in parallel with the resources they managed on these clients' behalf.

▶ ▶

PRACTICING THE COMMITMENT

MEDITATE. Do the Sufficiency Meditation each morning on one scarcity thought. Breathe for several minutes while seeing if you can find any experience other than enough in the now moment.

CHALLENGE BELIEFS. Identify your beliefs about scarcity. Apply the four questions from Byron Katie's *The Work* (**www.thework.com**), which is discussed further in Commitment 10. Check to see whether the scarcity thoughts are true.

DO BREATH WORK. Experiment with the physical contrast between scarcity and sufficiency. Hold your breath for as long as you can. Experience not having enough breath. Then breathe shallowly—almost as though you are panting like a dog. Notice the difference between no breath and some breath. And notice if there is a feeling of scarcity or "not enough." Then take deep belly breaths. Let yourself slow down your inhale and exhale. Be aware of the experience of fullness. Reflect on whether you were staying present in each moment of the breath work or anticipating a future moment.

PRACTICING
THE COMMITMENT (CONT)

NOTICE SPACE. Move through a crowded space and focus on the obstacles. This works particularly well in a busy airport. Approach your gate by trying to avoid people. Be in a hurry. Notice your thoughts and experiences. Then shift to placing all your attention on the gaps between people. Allow yourself to move into empty space. What is your experience of movement from this mental paradigm?

Note: This exercise also works if you are a snow skier (and are wearing a helmet!). Ski as fast as you can through the trees by trying to avoid the trees on one run, then moving yourself into the space between the trees the next run. Which one brings a feeling of ease? Where do you experience scarcity and sufficiency beliefs? How is the same run different or the same?

IN A NUTSHELL

For individuals committed to conscious leadership, the belief and experience of sufficiency creates a profound shift in their relationship with others and with life. These leaders shift to living life from a place of enough—not just for themselves, but for everyone.

CHAPTER SUMMARY

Having Enough of Everything

▶ Conscious leaders experience their lives as having enough of everything: time, money, love, energy, space, and resources.

▶ The scarcity belief that there is "not enough" causes leaders to focus on making sure they get what is "theirs."

▶ The myths that feed scarcity are that there is never enough, more is better, and it will always be this way.

▶ Conscious leaders notice this focus on the toxic myth of insufficiency and shift from a mentality of scarcity to one of sufficiency.

▶ To unwind scarcity, conscious leaders notice their reference point and check in with themselves, actively challenging their beliefs.

▶ Conscious leaders can practice checking in with their experience in the present moment, bringing attention to the physical body, and noticing the abundance of each moment.

▶ To those committed to conscious leadership, the belief and experience of sufficiency creates a profound shift in their relationship with others, work, and life.

Experiencing the World as an Ally

I commit to seeing all people and circumstances as allies that are perfectly suited to help me learn the most important things for my growth.

I commit to seeing other people and circumstances as obstacles and impediments to getting what I most want.

Suzanne worked in the manufacturing industry for years. After her son was born, she transitioned to a consulting practice and provided insight, analysis, and strategy for several clients in the industry. She excelled at her profession. When one of her largest clients announced an opening for the CEO position, she decided to toss her hat in the ring. She was convinced she'd be a great choice. She was well acquainted with the industry and had relationships with key suppliers and customers. Plus, having worked with the organization, she knew the players on the inside. She thought she'd be much happier engaging fully with one company as the CEO rather than consulting for many.

But during the interviewing process, it seemed that everyone was "out to get her." The headhunting firm wanted a blue-chip resume—which she didn't have. The interviewer asked unfair questions weighted toward other candidates. The board wouldn't acknowledge all the work she had done behind the scenes—they took credit for it themselves. And the other final candidate threw up one hurdle after another for Suzanne to overcome. It was impossible—the entire deck was stacked against her; she had too many enemies. And indeed, she didn't get the position. She was committed to seeing people and circumstances as keeping her from what she most wanted: the "right" job.

REACTIVE VS. CONSCIOUS LEADERS

The way leaders view people and circumstances dictates whether they are reactive or conscious. Reactive, "To Me" leaders like Suzanne see people as either on their side in getting what they want or obstacles. Virtually every leader we coach starts with this mindset. They are convinced they will feel happy once they get what they want.

But they're not getting it. People and circumstances are standing in their way. The capital markets aren't ready for their company to issue an IPO. The negotiating partner from the company they're trying to write a contract with has unreasonable terms. The person in charge of a huge company project doesn't have the skills to manage it on time and on budget. Whatever the reason, these "To Me" leaders can point to the person or situation that is preventing them from getting what they want. And typically, they either give up because the impediments are too difficult or, more likely, push harder to overcome them.

The wiring of our brain contributes to this "with me or against me" approach to life. One of the first things we learn to do is categorize. Ask young children to sort buttons, and they can separate the red ones from the blue ones. Ask them to separate shapes, and they can distinguish between squares and circles. This ability to differentiate is critical to navigating the world. If we weren't able to label and sort sensory data and life experiences, our brains would be overwhelmed.

The same skill becomes a disservice to leaders, however, when the judgments and categories get simplistic, entrenched and comparative. "People are either with me or against me, and either better than me or less than me—and I'll find evidence to prove it." It requires a lot of energy to constantly prove you are better than someone else. It's equally hard work to keep those you perceive as less than you below you.

Conscious leaders, on the other hand, are able to shift out of this state of comparison and competition to see everyone—including themselves—as equally valuable. Everyone is an ally in the bigger game of learning.

I commit to seeing all people and circumstances as allies that are perfectly suited to help me learn the most important things for my growth.

DEFINITION OF "ALLY"

Let's define "ally." Traditionally, allies associate with one another for some common cause or goal. For instance, we might unite in war against a common enemy. For our purposes, the common cause or goal we have with our allies is our individual learning and growth. Other people don't even have to consciously commit to being your ally. If you are committed to experiencing them that way, they are always instrumental to your growth.

Sometimes you can select this relationship—with a coach, forum group, or advisory board. We encourage you to go even further. Consider that all people support the discovery of an aspect of yourself that you could not have seen without them. Even the most adversarial—in fact, especially adversarial—individuals can help you grow or become aligned with what you most want to create. Every circumstance helps you uncover something new about your beliefs, behaviors, or desires. Every person or situation is "for you" in serving your learning and growth, nudging you to become more conscious. Again, if the universe is benevolent, always organizing for the highest good, then other people are part of this collective support for your personal growth.

By showing up in the world in this way, you can welcome everyone and everything as an ally. This means that the person on the other side of the negotiating table is a catalyst for learning about what you value and where you may have been overreaching. The inability of someone on the team to deliver his or her agreements offers valuable insight on your management skills or stubbornness to make a change earlier. No matter the situation, rather than wallowing in resistance, you can get curious and ultimately feel gratitude for whatever prompted you to wake up, deepen your consciousness, and grow as a leader.

THE ROLE OF CHALLENGE

In the experience of growth, pressure plays a critical role. Reactive leaders often revert to seeing obstacles when they encounter a challenge. Alternatively, conscious leaders welcome this experience because they see the benefit of pressure; it either causes them to wake up and take action or allows new things to come forth. Before something changes, it usually breaks down first. For example, athletes know that the workouts that make them faster are the ones that breakdown their muscles—literally tearing the muscle fibers—so they grow back stronger. Supportive pressure is a catalyst for learning, change, and growth. It challenges the leader to fulfill their potential and live in their full magnificence.

Birth is a good illustration of pressure in action. For a baby to be born, his head must exert pressure on the mother's cervix. Throughout labor, high-pressure contractions move the baby through the birth canal. Without this pressure, the cervix won't expand and the baby can't come through. Similarly, pressure is a catalyst for ideas to be born, and old systems to break down to make way for the new ones. We see Apple as a great example of being willing to let go of their best ideas to allow something new to emerge. For instance, the iPhone in many respects rendered the iPod—their prior best-seller—irrelevant.

THE COMMITMENT IN ACTION

Daphne Scott is a regional manager at a Athletico, a leading health care organization. Early in her career, she participated in many regional meetings. At the end of one of the meeting days, she received a devastating email from a top leader in the company: "Everyone is noticing your constant comments. People are even betting on how many times you'll speak." As the email continued to describe her behaviors, Daphne broke down sobbing; it was the most painful thing anyone had ever said to her. She believed the email tore her down, and that the author was thinking only of himself. She also thought he was trying to block her from progressing in the career that she loved. She thought he was mean and didn't value her intelligence.

Daphne noticed her thoughts and recommitted to conscious leadership. She took some time to get grounded, then called the leader who sent the email to ask for a meeting. She embraced him as an ally, regardless of him and his behavior, she shifted her perspective to believe that he sent the email because he cared about her. When they met, he did express his desire to help her. He shared with her that he wanted her to be a leader in the organization and that her meeting etiquette was keeping her from reaching her potential. While his comments might not have been phrased the way she preferred, he

> *Other people don't even have to consciously commit to being your ally. If you are committed to experiencing them that way, they are always instrumental to your growth.*

was helping her learn important things for her growth—both inside and outside her company.

This is a great example of shifting your perspective to cultivate a person as an ally. However, we want to be clear that someone's declaration that he or she is an ally is not what makes them an ally. It's neither their behavior nor their words; it is your choice of how you want to see them. Even if the author of the email did not consider himself an ally—he wanted Daphne fired and he did not support her growth—Daphne could still choose to see him as an ally for her learning.

For example, Peter is part of a highly charged team at a prominent Wall Street bank. His peers are not out for his well-being. They are out to step on him and over him. Peter chooses to see them as allies – here for his development and learning. He is learning not to be overly attached to outcomes, to trust in life in the midst of "obvious" opposition, and to invite healthy fear as a catalyst to wake-up and pay attention, rather than to be naïve. These are all choices he has made to view the circumstance as being for him and for his learning.

PRACTICING
THE COMMITMENT

When we consult with leaders working on this commitment, we ask them this key question: If the universe were using this person or situation as a perfect ally to help you grow, what would you get to learn about yourself and life?

Here are additional questions to help you shift your perspective to seeing every person and situation as an ally in learning. Before you start asking these questions, first ask yourself this question: "Would I be willing to see this person and these circumstances as an ally for my learning?" Your willingness is essential for any shifts to occur.

If yes...

- *What is it that I could not have experienced without this person/circumstance?*

- *What part of this am I most resistant to? Can I see that this is true about me? And am I willing to welcome/love that part in myself?*

- *What is my biggest judgment about the way it is? Am I willing to see that the opposite of my judgment is as true or truer?*

- *How is this person or circumstance helping me face something that I have been unwilling to acknowledge or face?*

- *What quality could not have been developed in me without this person/circumstance?*

- *How is the universe using this person or situation to give me feedback?*

- *How is this in service to my growth?*

- *What part of me is this bringing forward to welcome, honor, accept, or love?*

- *In twenty years (or two), what will I say I learned from that"?*

- *In twenty years (or two), what about this will I be grateful for?*

Here are some possible reasons you attracted this person or circumstance into your life:

- *You have judgments you want to release.*

- *This is a pattern you want to break.*

- *The universe is inviting you to pay attention to the wisdom in your body.*

- *You want to expand the possibility of who you can be and need the pressure of this situation or person.*

- *You want to discover where you are resisting in your life (physically, emotionally).*

- *You are learning to see your resistance and honor your "no."*

- *You have unexpressed emotions that you want to acknowledge or feel.*

- *There is something you've been unwilling to face.*

IN A NUTSHELL

Conscious leaders look at life through the perspective of learning and growth. They wonder about how everyone and everything—especially challenges and potential obstacles—are actually allies in their development.

Experiencing the World as an Ally

- ▶ Conscious leaders commit to seeing all people and circumstances as allies in their growth.

- ▶ Unconscious reactive leaders view other people and circumstances as obstacles to getting what they want.

- ▶ Most leaders start with this reactive mindset: they are convinced they will feel happy once they get what they want and if they can't get what they want, it's because others are standing in their way.

- ▶ Rather than seeing all people as allies, unconscious leaders think either/or: "people are either with me or against me."

- ▶ This does not mean that competition is nonexistent, but that even competitors are supportive catalysts for growth and that adversaries can be extremely beneficial.

▶ Challenges create the positive pressure often needed for conscious leaders to expand beyond the comfort zone and into their full magnificence.

▶ Conscious leaders are able to shift out of the state of comparison to see everyone and everything as equally valuable.

▶ This perspective recognizes that all people and circumstances are allies in learning and growth.

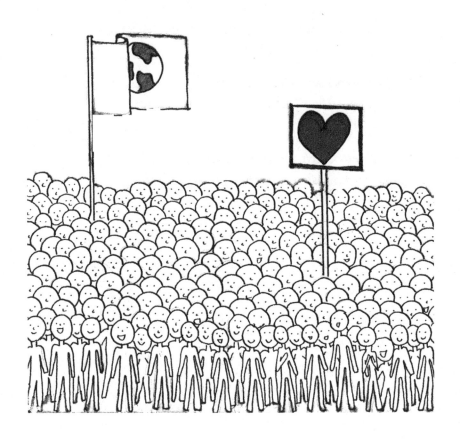

Creating Win for all Solutions

I commit to creating win-for-all solutions (win for me, win for the other person, win for the organization, and win for the whole) for whatever issues, problems, concerns, or opportunities life gives me.

I commit to seeing life as a zero-sum game, creating win/lose solutions for whatever issues, problems, concerns, or opportunities life gives me.

In early 2013, as we were about to write this chapter, our own partnership in The Conscious Leadership Group began undergoing some changes. We received feedback from our advisors that for a start-up to succeed, at least one person needed to have a passion for the organization: someone who would eat, sleep, and breathe the business and its vision. Both Jim and Diana felt inspired to become more and more committed to The Conscious Leadership Group and expand it as their primary activity. Kaley, meanwhile, acknowledged her desire to create products and content with Jim and Diana, but wanted to spend more time at home with her new baby daughter. Her lack of "burning desire" to devote time and energy to The Conscious Leadership Group seemed to be holding back its growth.

Like so many of the organizations we've worked with, we could have approached our situation with the following mindset: "It's a win/lose proposition. Either someone loses (win/lose) or everyone has to compromise (we all lose)." Those with this mentality believe that there are only winners and losers, and they must do everything possible to ensure that they're one of the winners.

WIN/LOSE, SCARCITY, AND COMPETITION

Scarcity beliefs lead to zero-sum, win/lose solutions. Many people think of life as a pie of fixed resources, for which they must compete with one another. Any money you have is money I don't get. Energy I use with you is energy I don't have available for someone else. Time does not increase (there are only twenty-four hours in a day), so the time you spend with your kids is time you don't spend at work. Any piece of the pie someone takes is a piece you don't get—everything is in competition with everything else.

In this zero-sum game, we must choose between competing and compromising. Competing means that I win and you lose. I get what I want and you don't get what you want—I get the position you sacrificed. Compromising means that neither of us gets what we really want, so we both lose. I don't get the deal terms best for me and you don't get the deal terms best for you; we both walk away disappointed.

In our experience, the most common form of problem solving uses this "To Me" form of negotiation. As a result, people miss creative solutions.

CREATING WIN FOR ALL

Another option for resolving issues is expressed in this commitment:

I commit to creating win-for-all solutions (win for me, win for the other person, win for the organization, and win for the whole) for whatever issues, problems, concerns, or opportunities life gives me.

From the To Me mindset, the only options available are competing and compromising. From the By Me mindset, a third option becomes available: collaboration. In our experience, collaboration opens all kinds of possibilities that are not available from competition and compromise.

This commitment is about collaboration. It involves many of the other fourteen commitments in an interdependent way. We used this approach to address the differing desires we had for our collaborative partnership.

CANDOR

First, we expressed ourselves with candor (Commitment 4). Jim identified his thoughts and feelings about the situation. And without blame, he invited Kaley into a conversation about her own thoughts, feelings, and preferences.

Conscious leaders approach solutions with full transparency and openness. They know that to create win-for-all solutions, they must be completely available and willing to reveal their own experiences with honesty and integrity.

SUFFICIENCY

We also focused on sufficiency (Commitment 12), staying open to the possibility that all our desires were possible. Because we had enough of everything, we didn't need to protect ourselves or compete for resources (like one another's time or respect). The content we had created thus far could be used in any of our work. We had plenty of internal and external support for each of our visions and independent consulting practices. Again, we believed that all of us could have what we wanted.

Conscious leaders interested in creating win-for-all solutions are committed to sufficiency. They not only believe but also directly experience that there are enough resources available for everyone.

SUPPORT

We also committed to support, to being allies for one another in our learning and growth (Commitment 13). Our conversation was open and explorative. The potential conflict was absolutely in service to each person's development and life path. It was an opportunity for all of us to look at our beliefs and patterns.

Conscious leaders who want to see win-for-all solutions experience every other entity as an ally in learning. Everyone and everything is co-creating an outcome perfectly designed for each learning path.

CURIOSITY

Finally, the three of us were committed to curiosity (Commitment 2), which lies at the root of win-for-all solutions. Most of the time, the answer isn't immediately obvious, and it often seems that desires are in opposition such that some people will be unable to get what they most want. By committing to curiosity, though, we cultivate a wondering about outcomes that are unavailable in just analytical thinking. This openness allows solutions to emerge that no one could have imagined.

Conscious leaders use curiosity as a tool for individual learning. In creating win-for-all solutions, they bring a deep commitment to curiosity to all their interactions; it underlies every conversation and experience.

In this field of candor, support, sufficiency, and curiosity, the three of us wondered about the next stage of The Conscious Leadership Group, while staying committed to a win for all solution.

As we revealed our experiences and asked for what we wanted in terms of support and sufficiency, we came to a solution that Kaley described as "absolutely the most perfect" for her. Diana breathed deeply, honoring what wanted to be. The answer involved an ending of the partnership in its old form.

We let our feelings flow and began to equate co-creating The Conscious Leadership Group with riding waves. Like surfers in the ocean, we had ridden the first wave together. Now, Kaley would sit the next wave out while Diana and Jim rode it. We committed to staying open to another wave that the three of us would ride together, or that another configuration of people might ride. This perspective allowed a win for each of us, for the community and movement of The Conscious Leadership Group, and for what we each imagined as the collective whole.

This isn't unique to our partnership. For example, one of our clients experienced an in-house conflict between the sales team and the product development team. The sales team was demanding that the development team design and produce products more quickly for their clients. The members of the product development team were angry because they felt they were being asked to produce at a pace that would yield subpar technology and ultimately disappoint clients. Of course, sales believed that they were losing clients because they were not responding to their requests fast enough.

We stepped in and supported each side in expressing themselves with candor, which included fully revealing their fear, sadness, and anger to one another. Secondly, we had them acknowledge their scarcity beliefs and encouraged them to work from the belief that they had enough clients, money, products, and time. Next, we invited them to see how members of the other team were allies, even though the feedback they were offering came in the form of criticism. Lastly, they got curious about how they could get their needs met in ways that supported one another.

The solution seemed obvious. The sales team recognized that they needed to do a better job of understanding the timelines required for developing new products so they could avoid overpromising to clients. They also decided that they could leverage their company's record for creating high-quality products, conveying to clients that they took more time to develop but were more reliable than the competition's.

The product development team recognized that their commitment to providing high-quality products had generated a mindset of excessive caution. They recognized that they could design new structures that would necessitate less oversight, which had been slowing down their delivery speed. They also agreed to go on sales calls to learn more about the challenges their sales colleagues were having with client demands, which created a great deal of empathy.

In the end, both teams created new structures that met everyone's needs. In doing so, they eliminated a lot of drama and used that energy to boost their competitive edge.

▶ ▶

ADDITIONAL WIN-FOR-ALL
COACHING QUESTIONS

Whether or not you do the process here, these questions (and questions like them) support the creation of win-for-all solutions:

1. Are we committed to seeing others as equals and allies in this collaboration?

2. What is the biggest idea that our teamwork could create?

3. What do we need to become to create this vision?

4. What do we need to let go of to create this vision (beliefs, attitudes, feelings, experiences)?

5. What resources do we already have that could support this vision?

6. Who else could join in this partnership?

7. How can our collaboration support us all to get what we want?

▶ ▶

PRACTICING
THE COMMITMENT

The following steps can help you create win-for-all solutions.
Keep in mind that the underpinning of this work is a
commitment to support, sufficiency, and curiosity.

Step 1: Identify the problem, issue, or challenge
For example; staffing, email, management style,
or conflicting desires.

Step 2: Get candid
Tell the whole truth about the issue from your perspective;
what is the issue behind the issue? Open a space for others to be
candid. Listen deeply to one another.

Step 3: Tell the story on the triangle
Identify victim-villain-hero dynamics and personas. Create
several win/lose, zero-sum solutions. Have different sides of the
issue win. See if you can make the solutions as egregiously unfair
as possible: one side "really" wins and one side "really" loses.

Step 4: See if you are willing to shift
Check in to see if you have a full body yes to create a win/win. If
the answer is no, stop the process and explore what emotions or
thoughts have not yet been faced, felt, or expressed.

If willing, go to Step 5.

PRACTICING
THE COMMITMENT (CONT)

Step 5: Claim 100% responsibility
Option: Do the 100% responsibility process
from Commitment 1.

Step 6: Get curious
Wonder about win-for-all solutions. (Do this while using
some of the shift moves: radically change your body position,
move, breathe, use other voices)

- *What resources do you have available that you
  haven't used?*

- *How else could you think about this?*

- *If you were the other party, what would you propose?*

**Step 7: Create an action plan to implement the new
win-for-all solution(s)**

IN A NUTSHELL

When conscious leaders experience an issue, problem,
dilemma, or challenge, they explore possibilities with
open curiosity and from a foundation of sufficiency
and support to arrive at win-for-all solutions.

CHAPTER SUMMARY
Creating Win for All Solutions

▶ Win-for-all solutions are a goal of conscious leaders and organizations.

▶ Conscious leaders commit to moving beyond the zero-sum game into a creative solution that serves all.

▶ Unconscious leaders see situations as win/lose and create a culture that promotes competition and compromise.

▶ Win-for-all solutions require the building blocks of the other conscious leadership commitments, providing a concrete example of how conscious leaders integrate all the commitments into a way of being in the world.

▶ Within an organization, win-for-all coaching questions help create a culture that supports and encourages everyone.

▶ The energy resulting from win-for-all collaboration allows solutions to be implemented quickly.

▶ A win-for-all culture allows an organization to thrive as creativity, collaboration, vision, and achievement are optimized.

Being the Resolution

I commit to being the resolution or
solution that is needed: seeing what is
missing in the world as an invitation to
become that which is required.

_I commit to responding to the needs of the
world with apathy or resentment and doing
nothing or assigning blame to others._

David is fifty-two years old. He made it. Twelve years ago,
he sat in a circle of CEO/President peers and announced
that he would retire at fifty and have a net worth "north
of $25 million." He also had a clear, compelling vision for
his company with benchmarks and deliverables. On the
home front, his goals were to "launch" his three kids and
figure out what he wanted to do with his marriage: get
out, get in, or stay the course. And he was going to lose
twenty-five pounds and get in the best shape of his life.

We talked with him recently after he returned from a bike
trip to Tuscany. The company is now under the capable
leadership of a new CEO. All the benchmarks were met
and the visions realized. He is north of $15 million (and
good with that). The kids are all in premier schools, he

just finished a fairly amicable divorce (he used to be north of $25 million), and his body fat has fallen to 13%.

Even though David "made it," we quickly recognized that something deep and meaningful was missing in his life. We were tipped off by the subjects he chose in our conversation and, more importantly, by the way he talked about them. Once he finished telling us about his latest adventure in Tuscany and the one before that in Morocco, once he talked about his wine collection and the people he had seen at the latest benefit ball, once he finished extolling the magnificence of his kids (with a slight tone of "despite their messed-up mother") and talking about the benefits of his latest workout routine, he switched to what was wrong in the world, especially what was wrong with our political system and the current economic policies. He went on and on about the lunacy and incompetence of Washington and the lack of "real leadership" in both the public and private sectors and especially in the world of education. He also talked about the failings of his favorite NFL team. On and on he went.

His energy would swing between apathy and resentment: "I've given up on them and quite frankly I don't care anymore. They're a lost cause."

David now spends most of his time assigning blame for what is happening in the world, whether in his personal world or the world at large. He is a living example of the "To Me" version of this commitment:

I commit to responding to the needs of the world with apathy or resentment and doing nothing or assigning blame to others.

David is not unique—extreme perhaps, but not unique. Leaders like him spend a lifetime solving problems, delivering results, and pulling people along. Many of them have done this from a To Me consciousness and particularly from the mode of hero on the victim-villain-hero drama triangle. Like other overfunctioning heroes, they have also spent their fair share of time in villain blaming and victim complaining.

This overfunctioning, typically caused by a deep desire for approval, control, and security as well as a strong belief that there isn't enough, eventually leads to a swing in the pendulum. And when it swings, it really swings. It swings from years (or months or days) of "caring too much and being too involved" (this is how leaders like David describe their former way of being) to caring too little and not being involved at all. Now apathetic, indifferent, and resentful, they develop a strong commitment (frequently based in entitlement) to do nothing except blame others or the system.

This To Me experience of apathy, indifference, resentment, and blame doesn't have to wait until we've "made it" to show up in our lives.

The apathy can show up in our view of "corporate". We hear people say, "At corporate they just don't get it—they waste money on non-value-added activities all the time. I've decided the best way to deal with them is to just not care. Talking to them is like talking to a brick wall."

We may hear parents say, "Quite frankly I've given up trying to help them. I've found the less I care, the less I get hurt. They've made their bed and now they can lie in it."

Or in our relationship with societal issues, like childhood obesity we hear, "I know it's a problem but there's nothing I can do about it. Do I really want to waste my energy taking on the cereal and soft drink industry?"

There are limitless ways in which we can look at the world's issues—or our own—and close our heart, harden our minds into cynicism, and check out into apathy. This is the To Me pattern.

BEING AND BECOMING

In our experience, this commitment offers an alternative:

I commit to being the resolution or solution that is needed: seeing what is missing in the world as an invitation to become that which is required.

Let's break down the statement and look at the words carefully.

This commitment begins with "seeing what is missing."

From our perspective, this does not mean seeing what is wrong or seeing a problem. We believe "problems" exist in the To Me box. Rather, something can be perfect but have a "missing" element. There is simply more that could be; there is more possibility, more magnificence, or contribution, or harmony, or alignment, or love. If we understand "missing" to be "lacking," we fall back into scarcity and the To Me consciousness.

A beautiful song with only one verse is not "wrong" or a "problem" or "lacking." It is simply that a second or third verse could add even more beauty. When we are "alone," we are not a "problem to be fixed;" if we had a partner, we might experience more.

When you look at your world, whether at work or in your personal life, what could be more? What is missing (not lacking)? What could be even more beautiful, efficient, aligned, or productive?

With this awareness, conscious leaders receive an "invitation"—not a demand or a responsibility or a "have to" or "should." An invitation comes with no obligations. You are free to accept or decline it. From this place of freedom, conscious leaders check to see if they have a whole body YES to the invitation. Again, this whole body yes is a master skill of all conscious leaders.

If leaders have a full YES to receiving the invitation to add to what is already whole, perfect, and complete, their next step is to "be" and "become." Please note: People often ask us, "If the world is whole, perfect, and complete, why would anyone ever want to do anything?" Our experience tells us that the answer is "because we can!" Because we can join in the creative dance. Because we can bring our gifts to a perfect world. Because we can write another verse to an already-beautiful song. This is what it means to be a human with freedom to take up the invitation.

Notice that we are talking about being and becoming, not doing. That doesn't mean there won't be doing. There often will be. But conscious leaders initially focus on who they are being and becoming. From this place, all action is possible. Action not rooted in beingness is usually short-lived, exhausting, and guilt producing (if I fail to do it). When "being" is prioritized, the doing happens naturally—just as an apple tree does not exert effort to give its fruit to the world. It knows its beingness and rests as apples come forward (doing).

This commitment doesn't point to just any kind of being and becoming. It specifically states "being the resolution" and "becoming that which is required." Whenever we sense that something is missing, the world invites us to be the resolution and become that which brings forth even more beauty, productivity, alignment, health, and contribution.

COMMITMENT IN ACTION

Let us present a very simple, practical example. An employee is walking across the ground of the corporate campus and notices several pieces of trash. If he is in To Me consciousness, he notices the trash and seeks to figure out who left it and resents the person for doing so, while either walking past the trash or picking it up and feeling resentful (this isn't my job) or prideful (I'm so good and so much better than the schmuck who left the trash). Or the employee does nothing because he is apathetic (it won't do any good to pick it up because it will just be back tomorrow, or I don't really care about beauty or even about the company for that matter. I'm just here to get a paycheck).

A By Me employee walks across the same corporate campus. He notices the trash and sees it and the rest of the physical space as perfect. Nothing "needs" to be fixed or changed. He hears an invitation, "Could our company be even more impeccable? Could we step into even more responsibility? Could these grounds be even more beautiful?" (These are just examples of many of the possible invitations the universe could give to a conscious person noticing trash.)

Next, he checks in to see if he wants to receive this invitation—does he have a whole body yes? In our experience, open, awake, and tuned-in people are always being invited by life to another possibility. They choose to accept some of these invitations and joyfully say no to others. Anything other than a whole body yes means no.

If he receives a YES, he takes a breath, drops into his center, and asks being/becoming questions like, "What would impeccability, responsibility, or beauty look like, feel like, or be like in this moment?" and "What is my current relationship to all three?"

When he allows himself to sit in these being questions, he finds himself naturally aligning with what would serve the world. As he steps into being the resolution and becoming that which is required around impeccability, responsibility, or beauty, he acts effortlessly. Many actions are possible, including picking up the trash. But he could also leave the trash and ask the person who left it to take responsibility by picking it up. Or he could speak to the building and grounds department about placing a trash receptacle there—and not just any trash receptacle but a beautiful one that fits the natural surroundings of the campus. From beingness, we have unlimited options for action. The By Me leader tunes in and does what is called for in that moment.

In practice, this several-step process becomes a way of living. Now a leader decides that communication is a missing element in his organization. Instead of blaming and complaining or throwing his hands up in exhausted apathy, he asks about his relationship to communication and asks what it would be like to be the resolution. From this beingness, he acts, not just once, but again and again. This act of responsible creativity is the benchmark of conscious leaders.

PRACTICING
THE COMMITMENT

Place your attention on your world at work or at home. Allow something that is "missing" to come to your attention. (If you see this "something that is missing" as a "lack" or "problem" go back to Commitments 10, 11 and 12 to shift your perspective.)

Is there an invitation in what is "missing?" An invitation is not an obligation, a should, a responsibility or a duty. This is an invitation you're really free to accept or reject. The invitation is to "be" and "become" something or someone that responds to what is "missing."

Check and see if you have a "whole body YES" to the invitation. If not, move on. If YES...

Ask yourself, "What is the universe inviting me to be or become in this moment related to what I perceive as missing?" Listen.

If there is "doing" that is to come forth from your being and becoming then go and do.

IN A NUTSHELL

Commitment 15 combines the mastery of several of the other commitments. As we become proficient in shifting from To Me to By Me consciousness, we move through our work and personal worlds seeing that everything is whole, perfect, and complete just as it is. There is no lack or problem. We can express our creativity in response to invitations from life to move what is in our world to even greater beauty, alignment, productivity, efficiency, and grace. For conscious leaders, this creative contribution flows effortlessly from the center of who they are. They are the resolution to what is missing in their world.

CHAPTER SUMMARY
Being the Resolution

▶ Being the resolution means that conscious leaders recognize what is missing in the world and view that as an invitation to become what is needed.

▶ When unconscious leaders grow weary of an intense version of the victim-villain-hero triangle, they often shift to an "indifferent" experience of drama, characterized by apathy and resentment.

▶ Many unconscious leaders, who have spent their entire careers problem-solving, delivering results, and pulling people along, often feel drained and want to disconnect.

▶ Team members who don't feel heard by unconscious leaders stop caring about making changes and give up on creating solutions that could benefit the organization.

▶ Conscious leaders see what is missing, not from a perspective of lack, but of opportunity. They then follow a calling to respond to the perceived need.

▶ Being the resolution takes place only from a conscious leader's whole body YES!

▶ Being the resolution incorporates the mastery of living from several of the other commitments and, once mastered, allows conscious leaders to move the world to greater beauty, alignment, productivity, efficiency, and grace.

THE CHANGE FORMULA
What About Tim?

Remember Tim from the introduction to the book?
When we left him, he was stressed out, unhealthy, and
unconscious, but commercially successful. Once he
stopped long enough to take in where he was going in
life—or more importantly, not going—and the stress and
anger he was feeling, he realized he needed to change.
We now return to Tim and his journey with conscious
leadership and shifting...

Tim is changing.

THE CHANGE FORMULA

One of the tools we teach our clients is the powerful change formula. Created by Richard Beckhard and David Gleicher and refined by Kathie Dannemiller (and quoted with permission by Dannemiller Tyson Associates) this formula can help you determine the likelihood of a change occurring:

$$(V \times D) + FS > R = C$$

C = CHANGE

"C" stands for "change," whether in an individual, a team, or an organization. It can be personal or professional: changing our exercise routine or our marriage, or changing an accounting system or a product-launch process. In Tim's case, he is changing the way he operates in the world—as a leader, a husband, a father, and a person. Let's examine each component of the formula as it relates to his transformation.

R = RESISTANCE

Change is about letting go of the known and stepping into the unknown. It is about releasing control and appears to always involve the possibility of "failure." The kind of change we talk about in this book—the kind that Tim is experiencing—is radical. It entails a total shift in how we are being in the world.

Like most of us, Tim is uncomfortable with change and resists it—the way he was being and what he was doing was "working." He was accomplishing many of his goals and, in his own words, he had created a life far beyond what he would have ever imagined. And, he had "a sense of control." We say sense of control because one of the things Tim is learning is that much of what he thought was under his control actually never was. His control plan was really an illusion.

This resistance to change is rooted in fear. Thinking about radical change triggers fear in almost all the leaders we've worked with—lots of fear. They are afraid of what they would risk if they changed. We don't shy away from this fear and we don't recommend that you do either. We invite you, as we did Tim, to ask yourself this question: "If I changed, what am I afraid would happen?" Or put another way, "What's at risk if I stop being the way I've been or doing what I've been doing?" Here are typical answers:

- *If I told the truth and stopped lying, I'd lose my marriage.*

- *If I dealt with my workaholism, I wouldn't get as much done.*

- *If I felt my feelings, I'd kill someone in anger or never stop crying or want to have sex with everyone I met.*

- *If I faced the fact that I'm not living in my genius but am just getting by in my zones of excellence and competence, my income would drop dramatically and I'd become a starving artist.*

- *If I began to see that the opposite of my story was as true as or truer than my story, I would lose all conviction and become a wimpy relativist who didn't stand for anything.*

- *If I started appreciating the people who work for me, they'd lose motivation and get a sense of entitlement.*

- *If I stopped living off adrenaline and started breathing, meditating, and sleeping, I "know" I'd lose my edge and get eaten by the sharks around me.*

Sound familiar? We occasionally meet a leader who says, "I love change. It excites me." But we discover that they're talking about change they initiate or change that allows them to stay in control. Someone might say, "I love eating at a different restaurant every night and going on a different vacation every year. Doing the same thing more than once is boring to me. I love variety. I switch jobs every twelve to eighteen months because I want newness. I constantly shake up my team. It keeps all of us on our toes."

This is not the change we're talking about. In fact, to people who are wired this way—loving newness and variety and hating routine and boredom—real change, the kind they would not be excited about and would likely fear, involves sitting in their boredom and examining the other side of it. Ask them to stay at home and sit still without distractions (computer, TV, reading material, music) for thirty minutes and their skin will start to crawl. Ask them to face their compulsion for newness, variety, and chaos, and they will tell you they'd rather be dead.

The change we discuss in this book alters a person's core pattern and identity. It shows up in our behavior but goes much deeper than that. All of us have adapted the best we can to make our lives work as well as they do. Shifting our identities and the beliefs that support them brings up resistance.

Back to the formula. To bring about change, something must be greater than our natural resistance. What is that something?

$$(V \times D) + FS$$

V = VISION

"V" stands for "vision," a picture of a preferable future. If people have a large, inspirational vision, it alone can motivate them to face their fears and step into and through their resistance. Great visionaries, like Martin Luther King Jr., Gandhi, Steve Jobs, Buckminster Fuller, Nelson Mandela, and others, can cast such inspirational visions that they motivate not only themselves but others to risk letting go of the familiar and stepping into a new way of being and doing.

When working with people and organizations, we spend considerable time exploring vision, using a process designed to connect people and teams to a picture of a preferable future. For vision to overcome our resistance to change, it must be real, heartfelt, deeply desired, and inspirational. Since the groundbreaking work of Jim Collins and books like *Built to Last* and *Good to Great*, many leaders and companies have come to know the value of vision, so they attend vision workshops. Unfortunately, the byproduct is often not inspired hearts, minds, and bodies, but rather an overly wordsmithed marketing slogan that is hung on a wall or inserted into a banner on a website. This type of vision will die in the face of resistance.

As Tim explored his vision deeply, he came to see that what he really wanted was freedom. He saw that although he had what looked like freedom, he was actually not very free at all. He was living in his own very elaborate and expensive prison. The more he envisioned what real freedom would be for him, the more motivated he became to confront his life.

Tim also had a vision for his connection with his kids. And he was concerned about the influence his way of being was having on them. He knew a deep connection was missing and he didn't want them to live the way he had (they were definitely on the path to becoming "human doings" and not "human beings"). He also didn't want his relationship with them to be transactional. He wanted to connect deeply with them, and wanted them to connect deeply with their own visions.

Tim had a vision for his legacy as well. Though he was successful at work, he knew that what he was building wouldn't last, that it wasn't sustainable.

Finally, Tim had a vision for more energy. He could remember when he had boundless energy and enthusiasm. Now he was constantly tired, often sick and never fully rested. He wasn't even having that much fun. Tim embraced a vision for an entirely different way of being.

How big is your vision? How motivational is your dream? What is it that you want, really want, that you can't attain by playing the same game? What is your picture of a future that is so compelling it motivates you to overcome your resistance to change, to let go of control and step into the unknown? The answer to these questions is fundamental to whether you will be a To Me or By Me leader. By Me leaders have compelling personal visions and By Me organizations have motivational, transpersonal visions that embolden others to take all the risks associated with change.

D = DISSATISFACTION

But having vision, even a deeply inspirational vision, is rarely enough. Most people do not change because of vision alone—they change because of pain. The "D" in the formula stands for "dissatisfaction," specifically dissatisfaction with the status quo. Most people and organizations overcome the resistance to change by becoming extremely dissatisfied with the status quo.

In most modern works on change theory and change management authors espouse some version of the "burning platform." The burning platform is another way of saying we have to be dissatisfied with the status quo because it isn't working and it won't work in the future. Most change theorists say that one of the roles of leaders in organizations is to create this burning platform. Burning platforms are necessary in most organizations and for most people because they create fear. In fact the purpose is to create enough fear and anxiety of not changing that it outweighs the fear of changing, the resistance.

In our experience, most To Me leaders avoid and anesthetize their dissatisfaction. They distract themselves by chasing the next bright and shining thing, whether it's a promotion, a new car, a new wife, or a new challenge. If that doesn't work, they numb themselves with alcohol, drugs, TV, sex, exercise, and all the other drifts identified in this book—anything to keep from fully facing and feeling the pain. What's interesting to observe is that the more successful leaders are, the more tools they have at their disposal for distraction and numbing. This is true of organizations as well.

Relationships at home and work are often a collective collusion to deny dissatisfaction and pain—one definition of codependency. They do this by not speaking candidly, believing that if they really tell the truth about their thoughts and feelings, chaos will ensue. They're afraid they would lose control and have to face their discomfort. They'd also quit protecting others from facing the truth of what is really going on in their lives. Here is how collective collusion in organizations and at home works: "I won't ask you to face your truth, pain, and dissatisfaction if you don't ask me to face mine." This unconscious agreement is a given in our culture and in relationships. It's a standard way of doing business. So when people in the system start telling the truth about themselves and others, they are typically ostracized and rejected for breaking the social contract. This courageous step, though, is often a gateway to allowing dissatisfaction to surface so real change can happen.

Tim's pain came from three sources. First, his wife told him that if they didn't change their marriage dynamics she was done. She didn't do this from a place of blaming Tim and making him wrong or bad. She actually did it from a place of 100% responsibility. Together, she said, they had created a relationship that was no longer working for her and she wanted to change it. If he was willing to work on the relationship, she was too. If not, she wanted out. None of this was a surprise to Tim but her willingness to say it out loud and not in an alcohol-induced tirade woke him up. He had a choice to make.

The second source of dissatisfaction and pain came from Tim's boss and mentor, who had a frank conversation with him. His boss told him that his intensity and drive had crossed the line and that he was now being perceived as a bully with an anger problem. This news actually surprised Tim. Throughout his career, he had received praise for his intensity, and now all of a sudden (at least it seemed sudden to him), his intensity had become a liability to advancement.

We have seen this many times. What was once valued as a real strength by the organization is now seen as a career limiter. This is a particularly eye-opening experience for the Tims of the world whose drive and intensity have defined their way of being. This realization creates pain and dissatisfaction because leaders like Tim don't know how else to be or how to change. It's like telling people who have thrown a ball right-handed all their lives that they now need to become ambidextrous if they're going to progress to the next level.

The third source of real dissatisfaction came from Tim's doctor, who told him that his lifestyle for the last several decades had taken its toll on his body. His immune system was breaking down and he now needed to take medication for his hypertension. If he didn't change his stress level, he was headed for heart disease and a stroke. The doctor also told him that his chronic back pain was probably more about his anger than anything physiological.

These wake-up calls didn't come all at once for Tim but over the course of months. The cumulative effect was a growing dissatisfaction and unavoidable pain. From our perspective, this was a good thing. The formula was working. Tim had pain and he had a vision. Although not a given, change was a real possibility.

How about you? How is your pain level? How much dissatisfaction are you experiencing? If you're like most people, you're still in the avoiding and numbing stage of pain management, and to some degree it's working for you. But for some of you, your defenses against facing reality are breaking down. Often this occurs in midlife. Some are fortunate to have this experience before their forties but many can insulate themselves until later in life. How are you denying your pain and dissatisfaction? What conversations are you avoiding with the important people in your life, and with yourself, so you can maintain the status quo?

Someone once told us that life first whispers to us in a still, small voice. If we don't listen, it speaks to us firmly, and if we avoid those words, it screams at us, often in the form of a crisis or suffering. Life tickles us first, pushes us second, and then hits us over the head with a brick. We are huge fans of getting our learnings in friendly and easy ways. This is probably because, like many of you, we have been hit with some hefty bricks.

Back to the formula. V and D (vision and dissatisfaction) are multiplied: V x D. Think of it as needing a hundred points of motivation to overcome R (resistance to change). This can come from a hundred points of vision and one point of pain or ten points of each. Again, for most people, the dissatisfaction/pain number usually far exceeds the vision number.

FS = FIRST STEPS

The expression V x D is like a car's engine. It creates the energy for propulsion, but without a drivetrain, that energy never gets to the wheels and the car sits still, stuck in place. Similarly, many leaders have the energy to change but no way to actualize it, so they remain stuck in place. They need FS, "first steps," the drivetrain that can put the energy of motivation into action (V x D + FS > R = C). V x D gives us the "why," while FS gives us the "what and how."

When Beckhard and Gleicher created the change formula and Dannemiller refined it, FS was used as a multiplier, just like V and D: V x D x FS > R = C. In our experience, this is not the case. First steps are not equal to vision and pain in their efficacy for overcoming resistance. They are necessary but not equal.

Many people focus on the "what" and "how" of change. As an excellent example of this, visit a local bookstore and look at all the books on dieting. They are loaded with practical and powerful first steps. The fact of the matter is that for most people, the FS of weight loss is not the missing piece, but rather V x D. That doesn't mean they don't have some vision and dissatisfaction—it just isn't enough. Likewise, the world is filled with many great how-to books on personal transformation and leadership, but they generate little traction and even fewer results.

Often when we coach leaders, they ask for the "how." It sounds something like, "I'd like to change, but I don't know how." We almost never trust this statement. Our experience is that where there is real willingness the how makes itself known. People avoid facing their lack of willingness by asking "how" questions. This is a subtle and significant trap because it keeps people thinking that they want to change – if they only knew how – and not facing their real resistance to change.

WILLINGNESS TO CHANGE

It all comes down to willingness. Willingness to change is very different from knowing how to change, or further still, truly wanting to change. Many, many people want to change, but most are not willing to change.

What in your life do you want to change? Make a list.

Now ask yourself, "Am I willing to change? Am I *really* willing to change?"

At this point, you might find yourself saying, "I'm willing but I don't know how." And we'd say that this is just an excuse to avoid your resistance. If you're like many of the people we work with, you'd get frustrated, even angry, when we challenge your willingness. But we don't do others or ourselves any favors by giving them temporary relief from their unwillingness to face their unwillingness. In fact, we think that one of a coach's core commitments is to lovingly hold pressure to help others confront their resistance.

Remember that the ego/identity is powerful (and that's good). It doesn't want to let go of control and step into the unknown. It equates control with security and safety. One way it most likes to stay in control is to allow us to think we're willing to change when we're really not.

You might also hear yourself say, "I'll try. I'll try to change." Our mentor and friend Hale Dwoskin says, "Trying is wanting credit for something you never intend to do." So true. When asked by friends if you'll stop by after work for a drink, you find yourself saying, "I've got a lot to do before I leave, and my kid is not feeling well, but I'll try." You want credit from your friends for "trying" but you never honestly plan to join them. You might even want to stop by, but the reality is that you're unwilling to go.

This is such a powerful part of our work that we took the 15 Commitments and turned them into willingness questions. When we coach leaders and teams, we often ask them these specific questions to support them in facing their unwillingness to change. Surprising things happen when a person owns their unwillingness and simply says, "I'm unwilling."

ARE YOU WILLING TO CHANGE?

Think of an issue in your life, one that you believe you want to change. Now read these questions slowly. Let them sink in and see if you can answer each of them with a whole body YES.

Are you willing to take 100% responsibility (not more or less than 100% responsibility) for this issue? Are you willing to stop blaming and criticizing others and yourself?

Are you willing to let go of being right? Are you willing to get more interested in learning than defending your ego?

Are you willing to feel all of your authentic feelings (fear, anger, sadness, joy, sexual feelings)?

Are you willing to reveal to others all of your withholds? Are you willing to speak unarguably? Are you willing to listen consciously to others?

Are you willing to stop all gossip about this issue? Are you willing to clear up all past issues with all relevant parties using the clearing model?

Are you willing to clean up all broken agreements related to this issue? Are you willing to renegotiate all agreements related to this issue that you no longer have a whole body

YES to keeping? Are you willing to only make agreements about which you have a whole body YES and around which you have control?

Are you willing to shift from entitlement to appreciation about this issue? Are you willing to place your attention on how this issue is here for your learning? Are you willing to let go of all past resentment and replace it with genuine appreciation?

Are you willing to let go of living in your zones of incompetence, competence, or excellence? What do you need to let go of to be willing to live in your zone of genius? Are you willing to live only in your genius?

Are you willing to let go of taking this issue seriously? Are you willing to treat this issue lightly and play with it? Are you willing to have this issue resolve easefully and effortlessly? Are you willing to honor your rhythms of rest and renewal, and sprint and recovery around this issue?

Are you willing to see that the opposite of your story is as true as or truer than your story?

Are you willing to welcome and release all wanting of approval, control, and security? Are you willing to experience no lack of approval, control, and security? Are you willing to let go of seeking approval, control, and security from the outside?

Are you willing to let go of beliefs in scarcity? Are you willing to experience that you have enough of everything?

Are you willing to quit playing a zero-sum game regarding this issue?

Are you willing to see that everyone and everything related to this issue are your allies?

Are you willing to let go of win/lose (competing) and lose/lose (compromising) views regarding this issue? Are you willing to create authentic win-for-all resolutions for this issue?

Are you willing to be the resolution that you are seeking regarding this issue?

Any answer other than a whole body YES reveals a lack of willingness. This is not a bad thing. The ego will want to make it bad, but it is not. It is just the suchness (as the Buddhists say) of where you are and it's perfect. Even so, if we don't face and own our resistance, we can stay stuck forever. We call it being in limbo: thinking we are willing yet not facing that we are really more committed to staying where we are than to shifting. We tell leaders all the time that the first step to willingness is owning— fully owning—our unwillingness.

When we own our resistance, we see that we simply need more motivation: more vision or dissatisfaction. This is not a problem. It is just what is so in this moment.

WILLINGNESS IN ACTION

Over time, Tim really became willing. He didn't just want to change—he was willing to change. All he needed was some FS.

For him, his first step was to find a good life coach who could support his transformation both in his marriage and in his relationship to intensity, anger, and stress. If you ask Tim to tell the story, he would say that even though he was willing, he was scared as he picked up the phone to call the coach for the first time—extremely scared. Keep in mind that willingness and fear usually go hand in hand. If you don't have some anxiety, you're probably not really willing to change, and you don't understand what it means to let go of control and step into the unknown. By Me, transformational leaders are always stepping into and through fear of the unknown. Get used to it.

Tim and his coach have spent the better part of the last three years facing, feeling, expressing, committing, and recommitting. Tim would tell you it has been a wild ride filled with all five core emotions (anger, fear, sadness, joy, and sexual feelings). It's been messy. We use the term toddling to describe this process. Toddling is what children do as they first learn to walk. It's actually somewhat of a controlled fall. They fall, get up, cry at times, shake it off, hold someone's hand, and get going again.

Others around him notice the change. Some relationships have ended, while others have developed marvelously. Tim has developed a number of new relationships with other By Me leaders at home and at work who support his growth.

For those of you like Tim, who are at a place of full willingness, meaning you have enough vision and pain to overcome the ego's natural resistance to change, we have included a chapter of next steps to support you in your journey.

To the rest of you, who are unwilling at this point, we say hurray! Willingness is actually no better than unwillingness, just as By Me is no better than To Me. They are just different states of consciousness and whatever state you're in, we believe it is perfect.

For those of you who struggle to see this as perfect, we understand. We encourage you to go through the practice of the "four A's." To begin, can you simply acknowledge that you are where you are? Acknowledgment is naming what is here and is a powerful first step. Now take the second step and see if you're willing to allow yourself to be just where you are. Third, can you accept yourself for being just the way you are? Acceptance adds a level of openness not present in allowing. Once you can accept where you are, see if you can take the fourth step. Can you appreciate yourself for being just where you are? Appreciation goes beyond acceptance into openhearted celebration. In other words, appreciation is loving yourself for being just where you are.

We all have an experience of this process. Imagine someone coming to your home. Acknowledgement is recognition that someone is standing at the door. Allowing is opening the door and letting them come in. It doesn't mean that I'm happy they are there; there is still resistance. Acceptance is relaxing into the reality that they are there; we both relax and kick our feet up. Appreciation is delighting in the reality they are there. There is nothing I want more than to experience this moment with this person.

As we said in the beginning of the book, Tim was a successful leader but unconscious. From our perspective and now Tim's, his way of being in the world was unsustainable and prevented him from experiencing all the possibilities life had to offer. Now that he has been practicing the 15 Commitments, Tim would tell you he is even more successful today and this success comes with greater ease and fun.

NEXT STEPS

When we present this material in person, people commonly ask, "What's next?"

IMPLEMENT THE 15 COMMITMENTS

For our corporate clients we answer this question in the form of a one to four year conscious leadership initiative which includes everything from specific daily practices, to learning partner exercises, team training, executive coaching, train the trainer and culture transformation. We have a very detailed methodology for implementing conscious leadership in organizations. If you're reading this book and you're interested in talking with us about how we can partner with your organization, feel free to contact us through our websites.

If you choose to start implementing conscious leadership in your organization we find that it works best if the leadership is on board with the vision. Again, these 15 Commitments are not business as usual and they will cause a shift in an organization. This shift is most friendly for everyone if the leaders are totally bought into the process and are practitioners of the commitments, embodying them in their lives, before they ask others to embrace them.

If you are asking how to apply this work personally, below are options we and others offer to support your growth.

VISIT OUR WEBSITES

Check out the Conscious Leadership Group website at **www.conscious.is** or the Kaley Klemp website at **www.kaleyklemp.com**. On both you will find community, information, support, tools, videos, courses and other materials that support your growth and development as a conscious leader.

CONNECT WITH OTHERS

Get connected with people who are committed to living the commitments of conscious leaders. Quite frankly, it's virtually impossible to live the commitments of conscious leadership on your own. As we have said all throughout this book, living these commitments is a radical way to live and we all need the support of conscious community to live radically in our lives professionally or personally.

CREATE A COMMUNITY

You don't need a large conscious community to start. You only need a few people who are committed to exploring conscious leading and living.

There are two ways to get a community, join one or create one. To create a community we suggest:

1. Start a book group using *The 15 Commitments of Conscious Leadership* as the first book you read. You will find other books you could explore in our resource list.

2. Give this book (or similar books recommended in our resource list) to a few people you would want to give and receive support from in leading and living consciously. Ask them to read the book and then get together and decide if you want to form a group.

3. Meet regularly (at least monthly) and use the facilitation guides and other materials on our websites to explore each of the 15 Commitments.

4. Make commitments and agreements with each other to practice what you are learning. Conscious leadership is not primarily an intellectual construct or set of ideas, rather it is a way of living in the world.

5. Invite others who are interested to join the group.

JOIN A FORUM

If you want to join a Conscious Leadership Group Forum we recommend:

1. Attend a foundation event sponsored by The Conscious Leadership Group. These are listed at **www.conscious.is**.

2. Join a Conscious Leadership Group Forum in your area.

WORK WITH A COACH

In addition to creating or joining a community, we
highly recommend that you get a conscious leadership
coach. The great thing about technology is that you can
be supported by some of the best coaches in the world
through the telephone or Skype.

Another coaching tip we give everyone is "eat your
own cooking first before you serve it to others." What
we mean is that it usually doesn't work very well to tell
other people they should do something before you are
doing it. In specific terms, we often see people who learn
about being above or below the line and then start telling
people in their world, "Hey, you're below the line! You
ought to shift." Rather than this approach, which rarely
is successful, we suggest that you master noticing when
you're below the line and shifting yourself. After a while
people will begin to notice a difference in you. When
they ask about the difference then you can tell them
what you're learning.

A FINAL APPRECIATION

We want to thank each and every one of you who has joined us in this great adventure. From our perspective, few things are as interesting as the conversation of conscious leadership. We invite you to live in this conversation and do so with a deep spirit of curiosity, appreciation, and playfulness. We stand alongside you and are delighted to be in that conversation with you!

RESOURCE LIST

All three of us love resources for growth. We imagine that many of you are like us. So, we want to recommend some of our favorite tools for growth in conscious leadership. We have grouped the resources in buckets based on the states of consciousness: By Me, Through Me, As Me.

BY ME

BOOKS

Allen, David. *Getting Things Done: The Art of Stress-Free Productivity.* New York, NY. Penguin Books. 2001.

Brown, Stuart, and Christopher Vaughan. *Play: How it Shapes the Brain, Opens the Imagination, and Invigorates the Soul.* New York, NY. Penguin Group. 2009.

Campbell, Susan. *Getting Real: Ten Truth Skills You Need to Live an Authentic Life.* Novato, CA. HJ Kramer/New World Library. 2001.

Chapman, Sam. *The No Gossip Zone: A No-Nonsense Guide to a Healthy, High-Performing Work Environment.* Naperville, IL. Sourcebooks, Inc. 2009.

Emerald, David. *The Power of TED* (*The Empowerment Dynamic).* Polaris Publishing Group. 2009.

Hendricks, Gay. *The Big Leap: Conquer Your Hidden Fear and Take Life to the Next Level.* New York, NY. HarperOne. 2010.

Hendricks, Gay and Kathlyn Hendricks. *Conscious Loving: The Journey to Co-Commitment.* New York, NY. Bantam. 1992.

Hendricks, Gay. *Conscious Living.* New York, NY. Harper Collins. 2009.

Katie, Byron. *Loving What Is.* New York, NY. Three Rivers Press. 2002.

Kegan, Robert, and Lisa Laskow Lahey. *Immunity to Change: How to Overcome it and Unlock the Potential in Yourself and Your Organization.* Boston, MA. Harvard Business School Publishing. 2009.

Kelly, Tim. *True Purpose: 12 Strategies for Discovering the Difference You Are Meant to Make.* Berkeley, CA. Transcendent Solutions Press. 2009.

Loehr, Jim, and Tony Schwartz. *The Power of Full Engagement: Managing Energy, Not Time, Is the Key to High Performance and Personal Renewal.* The Free Press. New York, NY. 2003.

Riso, Don, and Russ Hudson. *The Wisdom of the Enneagram: The Complete Guide to Psychological and Spiritual Growth for the Nine Personality Types.* New York, NY. Bantam Books. 1999.

Tolle, Eckhart. *The Power of Now: A Guide to Spiritual Enlightenment*. Novato, CA. New World Library. 1999.

Tolle, Eckhart. *A New Earth: Awakening to Your Life's Purpose*. New York, NY. Penguin Books. 2008.

Twist, Lynne, and Teresa Barker. *The Soul of Money: Reclaiming the Wealth of Our Inner Resources*. New York, NY. W.W.Norton & Co. 2003.

OTHER RESOURCES

The Enneagram Institute: **www.EnneagramInstitute.com**

The Hendricks Institute: **www.hendricks.com**

The Work of Byron Katie: **www.thework.com**

The Sedona Method: **www.sedona.com**

THROUGH ME

BOOKS

Bourgeault, Cynthia. *The Wisdom Way of Knowing: Reclaiming An Ancient Tradition to Awaken the Heart.* San Francisco, CA. Jossey-Bass. 2003.

Hendricks, Gay, and James Twyman. *Touching the Divine: How to Make Your Daily Life a Conversation with God.* Hay House. 2006.

Scharmer, C. Otto. *Theory U: Leading from the Future as It Emerges.* San Francisco, CA. Berrett-Koehler Publishers. 2009.

Scharmer, C. Otto. *Leading from the Emerging Future: From Ego-System to Eco-System Economies.* San Francisco, CA. Berrett-Koehler Publishers. 2013.

OTHER RESOURCES

Beckwith, Michael Bernard. *The Life Visioning Process: An Evolutionary Journey to Live as Divine Love.* Sounds True. 2008. CD.

AS ME

BOOKS

Dwoskin, Hale. *The Sedona Method: Your Key to Lasting Happiness, Success, Peace and Emotional Well-Being.* Sedona, AZ. Sedona Press. 2007.

Note: we recommend listening to the CDs as the best introduction to the Sedona Method. Please see Other Resources.

Greven, John. *Oneness: The Destination You Never Left.* Salisbury, UK. Non-Duality Press. 2005.

Rohr, Richard. *The Naked Now: Learning to See as the Mystics See.* Crossroad Publishing Co. 2009.

OTHER RESOURCES

The books and videos of Scott Kiloby:
www.LivingRealization.org/resources

The audio recordings of Hale Dwoskin and The Sedona Method: **www.sedona.com/programs.asp**

The basic Sedona Method Course: **www.sedona.com/store/the-sedona-method-4-in-1-supercourse-cd**

- *A 19 CD collection of Hale Dwoskin teaching the basics of the Sedona Method course.*

- *If you are new to the material, we recommend listening to the CDs, as opposed to reading the book, as it gives you a direct experience of the Sedona Method. However, the book is listed in the Books section as well.*

The Sedona Inner Circle 4 and 5: **www.sedona.com/all-products/inner-circle-volume-4-mp3**

- *A recording of nine-day retreat led by Hale Dwoskin that focused on helping people discover the truth of who they are.*
- *We recommend listening to the basic Sedona Method course before proceeding to the Sedona Inner Circle recordings.*

WHO WE ARE

CONSCIOUS LEADERSHIP GROUP

JIM DETHMER has been devoted to the practice of conscious leadership for 45 years. He has spoken to tens of thousands of people about how to lead and live from consciousness. He has coached Fortune 500 CEOs and their teams supporting them in transforming their lives and their cultures. He has worked with over 200 organizations led by entrepreneurs and professional managers across all industries. In addition to The 15 Commitments of Conscious Leadership Jim also co-authored *High Performing Investment Teams* (Wiley, 2006). When Jim is not working with clients you'll often find him at his soul's home in Northern Michigan playing golf with his wife Debbie and delighting in their six children and three grandchildren.

DIANA CHAPMAN has been a trusted advisor to over 700 organizational leaders and many of their teams. She is also a well-respected facilitator for YPO forums and chapters worldwide. Clients from Genentech to Yahoo value her clarity, compassion, ferocity and playfulness. She brings you to your edge and ignites your courage to step into the unknown where you can experience what you want the most. When Diana is not with her clients, you will likely find her gardening at her suburban farm in the Santa Cruz Mountains of California. She lives there with her husband of 25 years and their two children.

WHO WE ARE
KALEY WARNER KLEMP

 **KALEY WARNER KLEMP** is a sought-after speaker, certified YPO Forum Facilitator, and transformational executive coach. She advises senior executives on how to uncover and address core challenges and uses the 15 commitments to help high performing teams create conscious culture and superior results. Kaley is a master enneagram specialist, helping individuals and organizations outperform their competitors by unlocking a deeper understanding of what motivates and drives people. Prior to developing The 15 Commitments of Conscious Leadership, Kaley co-authored *The Drama-Free Office* and wrote *13 Guidelines for Effective Teams*.

● ●

CONSCIOUS LEADERSHIP GROUP

Conscious Leadership Group (CLG) is a movement committed to supporting the expansion of conscious leadership in the world by consulting with organizations, training through workshops and seminars and creating communities of leaders through Forums. To learn more about CLG visit us at **conscious.is**.

KALEY WARNER KLEMP

Kaley Warner Klemp leverages the 15 commitments with leaders and companies to provide a lasting impact and access to new levels of effectiveness. Find out more about Kaley at **kaleyklemp.com**.

INDEX

A

above the line, 18–20, 21, 22, 25, 27, 65–67, 74, 113, 114, 128, 326
acceptance, as one of four A's, 320, 321
accountability, 10
acknowledgement, as one of four A's, 320–321
action, willingness in, 319–321
addiction, 2, 9, 218, 219
adrenaline, 1, 2, 18, 26, 72, 73
Agape International Spiritual Center, 25
agreement(s)
    compared to commitments, 161
    defined, 159–160
    impeccable agreements, 161–165
    as one of four pillars of integrity, 159–161
ahas/aha moments, 99, 231
alignment, 155, 158, 295, 296
alive, fully, 2
Allen, David, 6, 163
allowing, as one of four A's, 320, 321
ally
    defined, 270–271
    experiencing world as, 266–277
amygdala, role of, 15–16
anger
    conscious vs. unconscious, 96
    if repressed/recycled, becomes mood of bitterness, 93
    issues with, 23
    learnings from, 95–96
    as one of five primary emotions, 85, 219, 319
    repression of, 89
    as sensation, 87, 88
anxiety, 1, 3
apathy, 93, 291, 292, 293–294, 298

Apple, 271–272

appreciation

    culture of, 98

    four elements of masterful appreciation, 183

    generating of, 174–187

as a gift, 181

    giving of, 181–182

    meaning of, 177–179

as one of four A's, 320, 321

refusing, 179–181

approval

    as one of three core wants, 237, 239

    sourcing of, 237–251

arguable statements, 123

artist/creator, as one of eight play personalities, 211

A's, four, 320, 321

As Me (way of leading), 26, 36–37, 39, 40, 335–336

"at the effect of" way of seeing the world, 28, 30, 31, 32, 36, 48, 49, 137, 177, 247, 255

Athletico, 54, 55, 56, 272

authentic feeling expression, 136

autopilot, 23, 24

awareness

    as one of three circles of candor, 119, 120, 123

    reflection of, 128

    self-awareness. See self-awareness

B

Barnett, Jim (case example), 225, 229–230, 231–233

Beckhard, Richard, 304, 313

Beckwith, Michael Bernard, 25, 33

becoming, being and, 294–296

being in the flow, 68, 69

being in the zone, 68, 69

being questions, 298

being right

    as primary commitment of unconscious leaders, 14, 64

Sarah (case example), 63

what's wrong with, 17–18

beliefs

    changing of/eliminating of, 53, 95

    as component of thoughts, 108

    development of, 112

    examination of beliefs that cause suffering, 228–229

    false beliefs, 193, 194

    judgments as revealing about, 113

    scarcity belief. See scarcity belief

    shifting of as bringing up resistance, 306

    wanting as leading to, 244

below the line, 13–15, 16–20, 21, 22, 25, 27, 28, 30, 65–67, 96, 97, 98, 112, 117, 326

"Best Stuff" exercise, 198–199

The Big Leap (G. Hendricks), 190, 194, 260

blame, 3, 24, 29, 45, 47–50, 51, 52, 67, 68, 96, 168, 177, 291

blame-shame-guilt interaction, 48

blind rage, 23

blind spots, 121, 128

Bolte-Taylor, Jill, 93

boredom, 85, 111, 306

breathing, 5, 67, 71, 92, 94, 96, 306

Brian (case example), 245–247

Brown, Stuart, 198, 206, 211

Buddhism, 318

Built to Last (Collins), 307

burning platform, 83, 309

By Me (way of leading), 27, 30–31, 32, 33, 34, 35, 36, 37, 38, 40, 50, 66, 179, 281, 297, 298, 309, 319–320, 331–333

C

cable news networks, and To Me way of leading, 29

caffeine, 2, 255

candor, 41, 107, 108, 111, 114, 116, 117, 118, 119–122, 123, 124, 125, 126, 127, 128, 129, 136, 144, 153, 154, 281–282, 283, 284

case examples

Brian, 245–247

Common Corp. 45–47, 49, 51

Daphne Scott, 272–273

David, 291–293

Diana, 76–77, 279, 283, 284

James Sabry Sr., 199

Jeff, 237–238, 240

Jim, 279, 281, 284

Jim Barnett, 224, 229–230, 231–233

Joe, 189–190

Judith, 139–140

Kaley, 209, 279, 281, 283, 284

Peter, 273

Sarah, 61–63, 76

Sharon, 5–10

Sue Heilbronner, 165, 168–171

Suzanne, 267–268

Tim, 1–4, 303, 304–305, 308, 311, 319, 321

Cawley, Dan, 220–221

celebration, culture of, 98

challenge, role of, 271–272

change

    in change formula (C), 304

    willingness to, 314–318

    change formula, 304–314

Christen, Pat, 184

circumstantial happiness, 98

Clearing model, 142, 144–145, 146–147

closeness, 5, 117, 193, 195

coach, working with, 326

co-creativity, 55

codependency, 310

cognitive/emotive loop, 90

collaboration, 8, 9, 18, 49, 99, 261, 281

collective creativity, 110

collector, as one of eight play personalities, 211

Collins, Jim, 307

Collinson, David, 214

commitment, defined, 19–20

Commitment 1: Taking Radical Responsibility, 46–59

Commitment 2: Learning through Curiosity, 61–79

Commitment 3: Feeling All Feelings, 81–105

Commitment 4: Speaking Candidly, 107–133

Commitment 5: Eliminating Gossip, 135–151

Commitment 6: Practicing Integrity, 153–173

Commitment 7: Generating Appreciation, 175–187

Commitment 8: Excelling in Your Zone of Genius, 189–203

Commitment 9: Living a Life of Play and Rest, 205–223

Commitment 10: Exploring the Opposite, 225–235

Commitment 11: Sourcing Approval, Control, and Security, 237–251

Commitment 12: Having Enough of Everything, 253–265

Commitment 13: Experiencing the World as an Ally, 267–277

Commitment 14: Creating Win for All Solutions, 279–288

Commitment 15: Being the Resolution, 291–301

commitment in action

Commitment 1: Taking Radical Responsibility, 54–55

Commitment 2: Learning through Curiosity, 76–78

Commitment 3: Feeling All Feelings, 99–102

Commitment 4: Speaking Candidly, 128–129

Commitment 5: Eliminating Gossip, 148

Commitment 6: Practicing Integrity, 165–171

Commitment 7: Generating Appreciation, 184–185

Commitment 8: Excelling in Your Zone of Genius, 199

Commitment 9: Living a Life of Play and Rest, 220

Commitment 11: Sourcing Approval, Control, and Security, 245–246

Commitment 13: Experiencing the World as an Ally, 272–273

Commitment 15: Being the Resolution, 296–298

commitments, compared to agreements, 161

Common Corp. (case example), 45–47, 49, 51

communication, as predictor of sustained success, 61

communication protocols, 7

comparison, scarcity and, 256–258

competence, as one of four zones, 190, 191–192

competition, 2, 206, 257, 258, 269, 280, 281

competitive juice, 3

competitor, as one of eight play personalities, 211

compulsive behaviors, 219

compulsivity, 2

concealing, 110–118, 153

conflict, listening to avoid, as filter, 126

congruence, 155, 156–157, 158, 159

connected relationship, 114

conscious anger, 96

conscious breathing, 71

conscious commitments, 116

conscious community, 324–325

conscious leaders

    as open and curious, 14

    as rare, 24

    Sharon (case example), 5–10

Conscious Leadership Foundation retreats, 62, 158, 165

Conscious Leadership Group (CLG), 61, 62, 76, 245, 279, 283, 284, 325

Conscious Leadership Group (CLG) Forum, 325

conscious leadership, website, 323, 324

conscious listening, 125

conscious principles, 258

conscious relationship, 114, 115, 116

"consciously creating with" way of seeing the world, 30, 31, 32

consciousness, defined, 218

content, vs. context, 20–22

control

    letting go of wanting to be in control, 35

    locus of, 51, 52

    as one of three core wants, 237, 239–240

    sourcing of, 237–251

core desires, 127, 239

core emotions, 84, 85–86, 87, 95, 100, 219, 319

core wants, 237, 239–240, 241, 242

correct, listening to, as filter, 126

creative solutions, 281

creativity, 9, 18, 36, 49, 50, 98, 99, 137, 156, 189, 190, 192, 194, 195, 213, 221, 245, 247. See also co-creativity; collective creativity; responsible creativity; sexual creativity

culture of entitlement, 176

curiosity, 8, 31, 32, 40, 53, 54, 55, 61–79, 115, 118, 123, 124, 129, 136, 140, 144, 283–285

curiosity/learning cultures, 57

cut and destroy actions, 95

D

Dannemiller, Kathie, 304, 313

David (case example), 291–293

deep breathing, 5

defend, listening to, as filter, 126

defense mechanisms, 47, 121, 218

defensiveness

posture and, 71–72

Sarah (case example), 62, 63

as trait of unconscious leader, 16

denial, 15, 96, 98, 218, 219

diagnose, listening to, as filter, 126

Diana (case example), 76–77, 279, 283, 284

directionality, 158

director, as one of eight play personalities, 211

discipline, in Four Ways of Being Model, 38–39

disengagement, 112, 156

dismissal (in refusing appreciation), 180

dissatisfaction, in change formula (D), 309–313

distortion, 15, 121

doing, compared to being and becoming, 296

downgrade (in refusing appreciation), 180

drama, 8

drama triangle, 70, 136, 228, 293

dream state, 217

dreamless sleep, 217

drifting, 69–70

Drift/Shift model, 67–69

drinks (alcohol), 4

drive, 3

drive-by interruptions, 7

Duggan, William, 212

Dwoskin, Hale, 37, 244–245, 315

E

Einstein, Albert, 53, 74

Einstein Time, 260

elephant in the room, 154

emotional intelligence (EQ), 82, 84, 86, 94, 100, 127

Emotional Intelligence (Goleman), 15

emotional literacy, 84–86, 87

emotional maturity, 87, 94

emotional wisdom, 94

emotion(s). See also feelings

as coming through body in waves, 94

core/primary emotions. See core emotions

defined, 84–85

duration of, 93

experiencing and expressing, 7, 90, 92, 93, 156, 157, 158

release of, 91–94

repressing and recycling of, 89–91

withholding of, 109, 111

employee disengagement, 156

employee engagement, 19, 111, 155

energy

abundance of, 118

blocked, 111

depletion of, 111, 117

flow of, 156, 158

as flow of life force, 110

integrity as facilitating flow of, 155

involved in gossiping, 136

management of, 155–156, 217

maximizing, 217

withholding of, 110

enough, experience of, 260–261

entitlement, 176, 177

everything, having enough of, 253–265

excellence, as one of four zones, 190, 192

exercises

"Best Stuff" exercise, 198–199

"Genius Email" exercise, 196–197

explorer, as one of eight play personalities, 211

expression, of emotions, 7, 90, 92, 93, 156, 157, 158

extrinsic motivation, 50

F

fact(s)

separating of from story, 142–144, 145

withholding of, 108, 111

fear

conscious vs. unconscious, 97

driven by, 2

as going hand in hand with willingness, 319

if repressed/recycled, becomes mood of anxiety, 93

learnings from, 96–97

as line that guards between zone of excellence and zone of genius, 192, 194

as one of five primary emotions, 85, 86, 219, 319

resistance to change as rooted in, 305

as sensation, 87, 88

toxic fear, 8, 47, 49, 50, 66, 97

unconscious fear, 23

as underneath all withholds, 124

feedback

blind spots about, 128

defined, 75–76

to Jason Hsu (case example), 128–129

reactions to, 17

to Sarah (case example), 62, 63
feelings. See also emotion(s)
feeling all feelings, 80–105
locating of, 86–88
as never mentioned, 3
release of, 89
as unarguable, 122, 123
wisdom of, 94–99
withholding of, 109, 111
fight, flee, freeze, or faint, 18
fight flight chemical cocktail, 71
figuring it out, 72–73
filters, 125, 126
first steps, in change formula (FS), 313–314
fix, listening to, as filter, 125
Ford, Henry, 214
forums, 325
four A's, 320
Four Ways of Being Model, 37, 38–39
Fuller, Buckminster, 307
fully alive, 2
functional relationships, contrasted with loving connections, 2

G

Gandhi, Mahatma, 307
Genentech Partnering, 199
genius
    areas of, 10
    as difficult to self-identify, 196
    expressing of as motivation, 50
    living in hers (Sharon), 6
    as one of four zones, 190, 195–196
    zone of, excelling in, 189–203
    zones of, understanding, 190
"Genius Email" exercise, 196–197
Genius Moments, 198

Getting Things Done: The Key to Stress-Free Productivity (Allen), 6, 163

Gleicher, David, 304, 313

Goleman, Dan, 15, 82

Good to Great (Collins), 307

gossip
  cleaning up of, 141
  compared to ping-pong game, 134
  defined, 134
  elimination of, 134–137
  handling of, 8
  at post-game debriefing ritual, 4
  reasons for, 138–140
  separating fact from story, 142–145
  when it's not, 140–141

Greenville Health System (GHS), 34

Gross, Bill, 206

guilt, 45, 47, 49, 50, 86, 206, 296

gut, as one of three centers of intelligence, 82, 94, 128

H

Haidt, Jonathon, 228

hand-off (in refusing appreciation), 180

happiness
  circumstantial happiness, 98
  in Four Ways of Being Model, 38–39
  role of, 19
  The Happiness Hypothesis (Haidt), 228

head, as one of three centers of intelligence, 82, 94, 127

health care, cost of, 19

heart, as one of three centers of intelligence, 82, 94, 127–128

Heilbronner, Sue (case example), 165, 168–171

Hendricks, Gay, 68, 87, 159, 190, 193, 194, 260

Hendricks, Kathlyn, 87, 159

heroes/heroing, 48

high-level problem solving, 18

HopeLab, 184, 185, 220

Hsu, Jason (case example), 128

humor, 210

hyperarousal, 18

I

if-only-ness, 241–242

implementation, of 15 commitments, 323–327

improvisation, 208–210

incompetence, as one of four zones, 190, 191

indifference, 293

influence, as predictor of sustained success, 61

information, as falling into three buckets, 75

inner critic interception (in refusing appreciation), 179

innovation, 9, 18, 49, 98, 99, 110, 123, 156, 213, 221

insecurity, 2

instinctive center, 128

integrity

    defined, 154, 156, 158

    four pillars of, 159

    practicing, 152–173

integrity breach, 154, 155, 156, 158, 165, 171

Integrity Inventory, 165–168

intelligence, three centers of, 82, 94, 127–128

intensity, pros and cons of, 311

intrinsic motivation, 50

invitation, compared to "have to" or "should," 295–296

iPhone, 272

iPod, 272

J

Jeff (case example), 237–238, 240

Jim (case example), 279, 281–282, 284

Jobs, Steve, 307

Joe (case example), 189–190

joints, 4

joker, as one of eight play personalities, 211

joy

learnings from, 98

as one of five primary emotions, 85, 86, 319

as sensation, 77, 87

judgment, 14, 86, 108, 112, 113–114, 115, 129, 138, 139, 143, 145, 183, 226, 269

Judith (case example), 139–140

K

Kaley (case example), 198, 209, 279, 281–282, 283, 284

Katie, Byron, 228–229, 230

Kaufman, Mark, 54, 55

kinesthete, as one of eight play personalities, 211

King, Martin Luther, Jr., 307

L

labels

as helpful, 269

life as not coming with, 227

as normal work of the brain, 112

of sensations, 86

language, succinct, as one of four elements of masterful appreciation, 183–184

laughter, 210

leadership, in Four Ways of Being Model, 38–39

leadership blindness, 17

leading

from above the line, 13–15. See also above the line

four ways of, 25–40

learning

combined with playing, 8

as primary commitment of conscious leaders, 14

learning agility, 61, 66

lethargy, 111

life force, 99, 110, 155, 156, 157, 158, 160, 194

life purpose, 158

"Life Visioning" (Beckwith), 33

limbo, 318

listening filters, 126, 128

locus of control, 51, 52

Loehr, Jim, 217

love

as motivation, 50

as underneath all candor, 124

lying, 107, 119

M

Mandela, Nelson, 307

matching, of experience and expression, 93, 156, 157, 158

meditation, 5, 213, 259, 261, 306

missing element, 295, 298

mistakes, 3

models

cautions with, 25

children and animals as role models for play, 207

Clearing model, 142, 144–145, 146–147

Drift/Shift model, 67–69

Four Ways of Being Model, 37, 38–39

Reveal/Conceal model, 111–112

simple black line as best model for conscious leadership, 13

money, 38–39, 255, 256

mood swings, 291, 293

moods, as consequence of repressing or recycling emotion, 93

"more is better" myth, 256, 258

motivation, levels of, 50

Murchison, Chris, 185

My Stroke of Insight (Bolte-Taylor), 93

myths, toxic myths of scarcity, 256, 258

N

naps, 212, 213, 214

NASA, 212

negative residue, 49, 50, 52

nervous system, as highly receptive to new programming, 195

Newtonian Time, 260

next steps, 323–327

non-duality, 36

nose-to-the-grindstone mentality, 205

O

oneness, 36–37, 39

openness, as one of three circles of candor, 119, 120, 123, 283

opinions, as component of thoughts, 108

opposite, exploration of, 224–235

out-there-ness, 241–242

overfunctioning, 293

P

pain level, 312

paradigms, 74, 116, 244

paradox, in leadership, 36

persona play, 214–216

personal "me," absence of, 37

personalize, listening to, as filter, 126

perspective, importance of, 259–260

Peter (case example), 273

pills, 4

PIMCO, 206

play

children and animals as role models for, 207

defined, 206–207

living life of play and rest, 205–223

as motivation, 50

persona play, 214–216

spirit of, 8

styles of, 210–212

Play (Brown), 198, 206, 211

play breaks, 212–214

play personalities, 211–212

post-game debriefing ritual, 4

posture, 71–72

The Power of Full Engagement (Schwartz and Loehr), 217

practicing the commitment

    Commitment 1: Taking Radical Responsibility, 56

    Commitment 2: Learning through Curiosity, 78

    Commitment 3: Feeling All Feelings, 103

    Commitment 4: Speaking Candidly, 130–151

    Commitment 5: Eliminating Gossip, 149

    Commitment 6: Practicing Integrity, 171

    Commitment 7: Generating Appreciation, 186

    Commitment 8: Excelling in Your Zone of Genius, 201–202

    Commitment 9: Living a Life of Play and Rest, 221

    Commitment 10: Exploring the Opposite, 234

    Commitment 11: Sourcing Approval, Control, and Security, 248

    Commitment 12: Having Enough of Everything, 263–264

    Commitment 13: Experiencing the World as an Ally, 274–275

    Commitment 14: Creating Win for All Solutions, 287–288

    Commitment 15: Being the Resolution, 299

presence, 67–68, 69

pressure, role of in growth, 271

projection, 113, 115–116, 121, 122

purpose, 32, 33, 38–39, 158

Q

questions

    being questions, 298

    in blame cultures, 57

    in curiosity/learning cultures, 57

    win-for-all coaching questions, 286

    wonder questions, 74–75, 101, 115

R

radical responsibility, 31, 45–58, 76, 115

reactive leaders, 268, 271

reactivity, 23, 24, 67, 70, 71

reality
> internal relationship to, 61
> seeing reality clearly, 107

reciprocation race (in refusing appreciation), 180–181

reflection of awareness, 128

relational disconnection, 111, 112, 113, 117

relational lethargy, 111

relational principle, 112

relationships
> functional, 2
> unconscious, 115

renewal, maximizing energy by honoring, 217

repression, 89–90, 91

Research Affiliates, 128, 129

resentment, 49, 291, 293

resistance, in change formula (R), 304–307

resolution, being the, 290–301

resource list, 331–333

responsibility
> in Four Ways of Being Model, 38
> taking of, 50–58

responsible creativity, 298

rest
> living life of play and rest, 205–223
> maximizing energy by honoring, 217

results, as form of feedback, 76

Reveal/Conceal model, 111–112

revealing, 110–118, 122–124, 128, 141–142, 153

rhythm, maximizing energy by honoring, 217

right, need to be, 53, 114, 144, 226

Riordan, Mike, 34

River Rouge plant, 214

Rock, David, 213–214

S

sabbath, 217

Sabry, James, Sr. (case example), 199

sadness

    if repressed/recycled, becomes mood of apathy, 93

    learnings from, 97

    as one of five primary emotions, 85, 86, 219, 319

    repression of, 89

    as sensation, 87, 88

safety, 239. See also security

Sarah (case example), 61, 76

scarcity

    and comparison, 256–258

    toxic myths of, 256

    in the workplace, 257–259

scarcity belief, 66, 253–255, 259, 280, 284

Schwartz, Tony, 217

Scott, Daphne (case example), 272–273

security

    as one of three core wants, 237, 239

    as rooted in something beyond performance, 8

sourcing of, 237–251

Sedona Method, 244–245

self-awareness, 15, 61, 67, 75–76

self-blame, 52

self-preservation, 64

sensations

    allowing, accepting, or appreciating, 92

    of emotions, 87–88

    feedback as form of, 75

    feelings as, 84, 85, 89, 91, 93

    intensity of, 85, 86

    locating and describing, 87

    locations of, 91–92

    as unarguable, 122, 123

    as waves, 94, 103

withholding of, 109

sensitive awareness, as first step of appreciation, 177–178

Separating Fact from Story model, 142

sexual creativity, 99

sexual energy, 86, 99

sexual feelings

    learnings from, 98–99

    as one of five primary emotions, 85, 86, 319

    repression of, 89

    as sensation, 87, 88

sexual lust, as differentiated from sexual creativity, 99

shame, 8, 45, 47, 49, 50, 67, 160

Sharon (case example), 4

shift moves, 20, 71, 72, 75, 144

shifting, 17–18, 27, 40, 67–69, 70, 71–72, 254, 260, 273, 306, 318, 326

simple black line, as best model for conscious leadership, 13

sincerity, as one of four elements of masterful appreciation, 183

sleep, 1, 217

sleep deprived, 1

something happens, 68–69, 193

The Soul of Money (Twist), 255, 261

Sounds True, 33

Source, words for, 66

speaking candidly, 106–133

speaking unarguably, 122

specificity, as one of four elements of masterful appreciation, 183

spinners, 3

story, separating fact from, 142–144, 145

storyteller, as one of three centers of intelligence, 212

Strategic Intuition: The Creative Spark in Human Achievement (Duggan), 212

succinct language, as one of four elements of masterful appreciation, 183–184

suchness, 226, 318

sufficiency, 253, 261, 282

sufficiency meditation, 261–263

sugar, 2

support, 282–283

surrender, 27, 34, 35, 36, 37, 38

survival, 16–18, 64, 65, 66, 67, 239, 243, 245

Suzanne (case example), 267–268

T

Taking 100% Responsibilities Worksheet, 56

teams, importance of, 117

"that's just the way it is" myth, 256, 258

"there is never enough" myth, 256, 258

thoughts

    as comprised of beliefs, judgments, and opinions, 108

    as unarguable, 122, 123

    withholding of, 108, 111

threats, for today's leaders, 16

3M, 213

Through Me (way of leading), 27, 31–36, 37, 39, 40, 334

Tim (case example), 1–4, 303, 304–305, 308, 311, 319–320, 321

time, in Four Ways of Being Model, 38–39

To Me (way of leading), 26, 27, 28–29, 30, 31, 32, 35, 36, 37, 38, 40, 50, 51, 66, 83, 122, 177, 268, 269, 281, 293, 294, 295, 296, 309, 320

toddling, 319

toxic fear, 8, 47, 49, 50, 66, 97

toxic myths of scarcity, 256

transformation, 67

truth, ability to tell selves, as mark of conscious leaders, 15, 20

truthfulness, as one of three circles of candor, 119, 120, 123

Turn Inc., 224

turnaround, 229, 231

Twelve Step movement, 122

Twist, Lynne, 255, 256, 259, 260

type As, 3

tyranny of the urgent, 9

U

ultimate zone, 195

unarguable statements, 123

unarguable truth, as one of four elements of masterful appreciation, 183

uncaused joy, 98

unconscious anger, 96

unconscious leaders

    as closed and defensive, 14

    defined, 23

    Tim (case example). See Tim (case example)

unconscious relationships, 115

uninformed, 119

upper limits, 192–193

Upper Limits Problem, 193–195

V

value, increase in, as second step in appreciation, 179

victim consciousness, 29, 30, 32

victims, 48, 49

victim-villain-hero triangle/mode, 49, 54, 55, 177

villains, 48, 49

vision

    in change formula (V), 307–309

    in general, 32, 34–35

W

waking state, 217

wanting to be right, 15, 18, 64–65, 228

wants

    core wants, 237, 239–240, 241, 242

    issues as, 238

wanting is the issue, not the wants, 243

Warner, Jim, 198

Welch, Jack, 107, 117

whole body YES/full YES, 162, 163, 164, 165, 169, 295, 297, 316–317, 318

wholeness, 155, 156, 157, 158, 159, 165, 261

willingness

    in action, 319–321

    to change, 314–318

    as going hand in hand with fear, 319

win-for-all coaching questions, 286

win-for-all solutions, 278–289

win/lose solutions, 279, 280

"with me or against me" approach, 269

withdrawing, 112, 113, 121

withholding, 107–110, 117, 119, 124, 128, 153

wonder, state of, 72–75

wonder questions, 73–75, 101, 115

word cloud, 184

workaholism, 218–219

The Work by Byron Katie, 228, 229, 230, 233

world

    experiencing of as ally, 266–277

    looking at issues in, 294–295

    as showing up, 53

way it should be/way it shouldn't be, 52

Y

Yerkes-Dodson effect, 18

YES, whole body/full, 162, 163, 164, 165, 169, 295, 297, 316–317, 318

YES AND, 208–209

yoga, 6

Your Brain at Work (Rock), 213

Z

zero-sum game, 279, 280

zone of genius

excelling in, 189–203

false beliefs as keeping from moving into, 193

fear as line guarding between zone of excellence and zone of genius, 192, 193

understanding, 190

Made in the USA
Monee, IL
30 April 2021

67279004R00218